MANUFACTURING BY AI
AI *Road Map to Smart Factories*

by Sayeed Siddiqui

Dedication Page

To the thinkers, builders, and dreamers of a better industry—
 May this roadmap guide your steps into a smarter, more ethical future.

And to Arpita Arya

Introduction

- From Concept to Capability

Chapter 1: Foundations of AI in Manufacturing

- Defining Industry 4.0

- Role of AI in Modern Factories

- Core Technologies and Infrastructure

Chapter 2: Data as the New Raw Material

- Sensor Networks and IoT

- Data Lakes and Integration

- Analytics and Feedback Loops

Chapter 3: Predictive Maintenance and Asset Intelligence

- Machine Learning for Failure Prediction

- Smart Maintenance Scheduling

- Tools, Platforms, and Case Studies

Chapter 4: Quality Control and Process Optimization

- Vision-Based Inspection Systems

- AI for Yield and Waste Reduction

- Case Applications and Metrics

Chapter 5: Supply Chain Intelligence

- Forecasting Demand with AI

- Supplier Risk and Inventory Optimization

- Autonomous Fulfillment and Procurement

Chapter 6: AI on the Factory Floor: Operations and Automation

- Predictive Operations and Scheduling

- Process Optimization and Self-Tuning Lines

- Computer Vision and Intelligent Inspection

- Collaborative Robotics and Human-AI Interaction

- Autonomous Material Handling and Smart Logistics

- Digital Twins and Real-Time Factory Intelligence

- The Intelligent Factory in Action

Chapter 7: AI in Enterprise Decision-Making and Strategic Integration

- Strategic Planning and Executive Simulation

- AI in Finance, Forecasting, and Investment

- AI for Product Design and Innovation

- ESG, Sustainability, and Responsible AI

- Enterprise-Wide AI Integration

Chapter 8: Scaling AI — Governance, Talent, and Enterprise Architecture

- AI Governance: Ethics, Compliance, and Control

- Building Talent and AI Fluency

- ModelOps and Scalable Architecture

- Maturity Models and Transformation Roadmap

Chapter 9: The Future of Intelligent Manufacturing

- Vision of the Next Industrial Age

- Emerging Trends and Technologies

- Ethical AI and Social Responsibility

- Leading the Intelligent Enterprise

Back Matter

- Glossary

- Index

- Acknowledgments

- About the Author

1.0 The Shift from Automation to Intelligence

Manufacturing has always been more than an economic activity—it is a mirror of human progress. From ancient blacksmiths forging tools by hand to the sprawling smart factories of today, each evolutionary phase has reflected the priorities, capacities, and imagination of its time. The 21st century marks a pivotal shift—not simply in how we make things, but in how those things are conceived, adapted, and improved in real time. This shift is not merely a matter of efficiency or cost savings—it is a revolution in thought, agency, and intelligence.

In prior revolutions, machines were designed to follow commands. They executed pre-programmed instructions, often tirelessly, and often without deviation. Whether a hydraulic press or a programmable logic controller (PLC), traditional automation has relied on determinism—a predefined logic of input and output. While this approach powered the boom of mass manufacturing in the 20th century, it lacked the ability to sense context, learn from performance, or correct itself dynamically.

Now, a new paradigm is emerging—one in which machines no longer need to be told exactly what to do. Instead, they learn, adapt, and act on their own. This is the promise of artificial intelligence (AI) in manufacturing: not just faster machines, but *thinking systems*.

At the heart of this transformation lies the difference between **automation** and **autonomy**. Automation is rules-based; it repeats a fixed behavior endlessly. Autonomy is learning-based; it modifies behavior based on evolving data. Imagine a robot arm on an assembly line: in the automation era, it repeats the same motion, regardless of wear or variation in parts. In the AI-driven era, that same robot uses sensors and algorithms to detect micro-changes in part alignment, predicts the chance of failure, and self-adjusts to maintain optimal performance.

This leap from reactive to proactive, from passive to perceptive, is redefining the DNA of manufacturing.

The implications of this shift are profound. First, decision-making is moving from the boardroom to the shop floor. In traditional factories, any anomaly or optimization typically required human intervention. A quality control issue, for instance, would be detected hours after production. Now, with real-time AI analytics, systems can detect anomalies within seconds, isolate the root cause, and reconfigure parameters on the fly—sometimes before a human is even aware of the deviation.

Second, the factory is becoming more than just a physical space—it is a cognitive environment. Machines communicate with one another. Systems integrate across departments—engineering, logistics, procurement, and customer service. Through AI, a delay in raw material delivery can trigger a cascade of rescheduling, production optimization, and real-time customer notification—without a single human triggering the process.

Third, this intelligence is not limited to the machines alone. Operators, engineers, planners, and executives are all increasingly augmented by AI tools. From dynamic production planning dashboards to AI-powered maintenance advisors and real-time supply risk alerts, the human workforce is gaining unprecedented visibility and predictive foresight.

In this context, AI is not replacing the workforce—it is *elevating* it. Tasks once manual, repetitive, or cognitively taxing are now being reassigned to machines. Humans, freed from rote responsibilities, can focus on strategy, innovation, and collaboration.

Perhaps most importantly, the intelligent factory is no longer a vision of the future—it is a reality.

Around the world, AI is already embedded in industrial plants, silently optimizing line speed, reducing waste, detecting micro-defects, and guiding supply chain decisions. Companies adopting AI-first manufacturing models are not only seeing productivity gains—they are also reporting greater agility, resilience, and customer satisfaction.

The rise of AI in manufacturing marks more than a technological shift—it represents a redefinition of industrial philosophy. We are moving from *mechanical repetition* to *dynamic cognition*, from *mass production* to *mass customization*, and from *human-controlled processes* to *human–machine partnerships*.

This chapter—and this book—aim to explore this transformation in full. From predictive maintenance to generative design, from AI-powered robotics to real-time analytics, we will explore how manufacturing is being reimagined from the ground up. Not every company will embrace this change at the same speed, but one thing is certain: those who do not adapt will be left behind.

The future of manufacturing is not about producing more. It is about producing smarter, cleaner, faster—and above all, more intelligently.

1.1 A Brief History of Industrial Evolution

To understand the significance of artificial intelligence in manufacturing today, we must first retrace the path that brought us here. The evolution of industrial production has never been linear—it has been marked by distinct revolutions, each catalyzed by groundbreaking technologies that fundamentally reshaped economies, societies, and human roles.

Each industrial revolution not only introduced new machinery but also reshaped how value was created, how people worked, and how nations developed. These weren't just upgrades in equipment—they were paradigm shifts in civilization.

Industry 1.0 – Mechanization and the Age of Steam (Late 18th Century)

The first industrial revolution began in the late 1700s and was powered by steam and water. Textile manufacturing was among the earliest industries to mechanize, with inventions like the spinning jenny, water frame, and power loom turning cottage industries into factory-based production systems. Steam engines powered early railways and ships, bringing newfound speed to transportation and commerce.

This revolution was deeply labor-intensive, and while it replaced certain types of manual labor, it also created new classes of skilled machinists and operators. Cities grew rapidly as workers moved toward industrial hubs.

Industry 2.0 – Electrification and Mass Production (Late 19th to Early 20th Century)

The second revolution, occurring between 1870 and 1914, was driven by electricity. Unlike steam, which required close proximity to a power source, electricity enabled flexible factory layouts and introduced lighting, reducing dependency on daylight.

One of the most iconic transformations of this era was the assembly line, perfected by Henry Ford in 1913. This innovation drastically reduced the time to manufacture a car—from over 12 hours to just 93 minutes. Interchangeable parts and division of labor made mass production possible and profitable.

Beyond manufacturing, this era marked the rise of labor unions, scientific management, and early multinational corporations. It also laid the groundwork for consumer culture, as products became more affordable and widely available.

Industry 3.0 – Digitization and Automation (1970s to Early 2000s)

The third industrial revolution began in the post–World War II era and accelerated during the 1970s. It was characterized by the rise of electronics, digital systems, and automation technologies.

Microprocessors, programmable logic controllers (PLCs), and computer numerical control (CNC) machines allowed manufacturers to automate tasks that once required human oversight. For the first time, logic and feedback loops could be built directly into machines.

Factories became cleaner, faster, and more precise. Lean manufacturing principles, Six Sigma quality control, and ERP systems emerged, enabling global supply chains and just-in-time production models. Japan, in particular, became a leader in quality-driven manufacturing, with Toyota's production system becoming a global benchmark.

Digitization also began to decentralize intelligence in the plant. Tasks that once needed large centralized control rooms could be handled by distributed control systems and SCADA interfaces. It was the beginning of intelligent automation, but still largely rule-based.

Industry 4.0 – Intelligence, Interconnectivity, and Autonomy (2010s–Present)

The fourth industrial revolution—often referred to as Industry 4.0—is the most profound transformation yet. Unlike previous eras, which improved physical performance, Industry 4.0 infuses digital intelligence into the physical world. This convergence of information technology (IT) and operational technology (OT) enables machines to *sense*, *analyze*, *predict*, and even *decide* autonomously.

The foundational technologies of Industry 4.0 include:

- **Artificial Intelligence and Machine Learning**

- **Industrial Internet of Things (IIoT)**

- **Big Data and Advanced Analytics**

- **Edge and Cloud Computing**

- **Cyber-Physical Systems**

- **Digital Twins**

- **Augmented Reality (AR) and Virtual Reality (VR)**

- **5G and Real-Time Communication Networks**

This revolution is not merely about doing things faster or cheaper. It's about doing them *smarter*, *cleaner*, and more *resiliently*. It enables mass customization, ultra-flexible manufacturing, predictive maintenance, energy efficiency, and continuous process optimization.

Where the third revolution automated the *task*, Industry 4.0 automates the *thinking* around the task.

Historical Comparison Snapshot

Revolution	Main Driver	Factory Model	Workforce Impact	Notable Innovation
1.0	Steam & Water Power	Mechanized Craftsmanship	Shift from artisan to operator	Spinning Jenny, Steam Engine
2.0	Electricity	Mass Produc	Rise of the	Conveyor

		tion & Assembly	blue-collar worker	Belt, Electric Motor
3.0	Electronics & IT	Automated Production	Rise of white-collar engineers	PLCs, CNCs, ERP Systems
4.0	AI & Connectivity	Intelligent Factories	Rise of data scientists, hybrid roles	Digital Twin, IIoT, AI

Conclusion: Why This History Matters

Understanding the trajectory of these revolutions is not just academic—it is strategic. Every previous industrial leap created winners and losers. Those who embraced change, adapted quickly, and invested early in new capabilities consistently emerged as leaders.

Today, the transition to AI is following the same historical arc—but with far more speed. What took decades in the past now unfolds in just a few years. Those who understand this context are better prepared to navigate the future—and that is exactly what this book aims to equip you for.

Up next, we will define the building blocks of AI in manufacturing, demystify the terminology, and explore what it really means to have *intelligent* systems running a factory.

1.2 What Is Artificial Intelligence in Manufacturing?

Artificial Intelligence (AI) is one of the most transformative technologies of the 21st century, but its meaning often varies depending on the context. In everyday language, AI is the simulation of human intelligence by machines. In manufacturing, however, AI goes far beyond chatbots or language models—it refers to a collection of intelligent systems that can perceive, learn, analyze, and act in ways that optimize industrial processes.

Let's break this down practically.

Imagine a traditional automated conveyor belt. It moves at a set speed, responds to limited triggers (e.g., a sensor detecting a blockage), and follows fixed logic. Now imagine a smart conveyor belt that learns over time which sections slow down during certain shifts, which components tend to fail at what hours, and which product batches need gentler handling. This smart conveyor adjusts itself continuously based on real-time data—*without waiting for human input*.

That's AI in action.

The Core Capabilities of AI in Manufacturing

AI isn't a single tool. It's a suite of technologies and techniques. Each plays a role in turning raw data into intelligent, automated decisions that directly impact manufacturing efficiency, quality, and adaptability.

1. Machine Learning (ML)

Machine Learning is the backbone of most AI systems. ML algorithms learn patterns from historical data and use those patterns to make predictions or decisions. In manufacturing, ML is used to:

- Predict machine failures based on past maintenance data

- Forecast product demand from seasonal sales patterns

- Identify anomalies in production runs

- Optimize energy usage across shifts

There are three main types of ML used in factories:

- **Supervised Learning:** Where models are trained on labeled data (e.g., past records of defective and non-defective parts).

- **Unsupervised Learning:** Used to discover hidden patterns in unlabeled data (e.g., clustering product types based on similarities).

- **Reinforcement Learning:** Systems learn by trial and error to achieve the best result (used in robotics and process optimization).

2. Deep Learning

Deep learning is a subset of ML that uses artificial neural networks to mimic how the human brain processes information. It's particularly useful when working with complex, high-dimensional data like images or audio.

Example: A deep learning model can detect surface defects on metal sheets, even when those defects are subtle, irregular, or previously unseen. The system gets better over time by learning from thousands of examples.

Deep learning is behind much of the progress in **computer vision**, **speech recognition**, and **sensor fusion**.

3. Computer Vision

One of the most tangible and impactful applications of AI in manufacturing is computer vision. It allows machines to "see" and interpret visual information.

- Real-time part inspection at assembly lines

- Optical character recognition (OCR) for label verification

- Robot guidance for precise pick-and-place operations

- Surface quality analysis for painted or coated components

Computer vision systems often outperform human inspectors in both speed and accuracy. Unlike humans, they don't suffer from fatigue or inconsistency.

4. Natural Language Processing (NLP)

Manufacturing isn't just about machines; it's also about information—most of which exists in unstructured forms like maintenance logs, shift reports, operator notes, or technical manuals.

Natural Language Processing allows systems to understand, categorize, and even generate human language.

Use cases:

- Automatically tagging and routing service tickets

- Extracting failure patterns from maintenance logs

- Enabling voice-activated systems for operators on the floor

Some advanced NLP systems are now integrated with digital assistants in factories, allowing supervisors to query real-time data using conversational commands.

5. Reinforcement Learning

Reinforcement Learning (RL) is an AI approach where an agent learns by interacting with its environment, receiving feedback (rewards or penalties), and improving over time.

This is particularly useful in scenarios where:

- The environment is dynamic

- The ideal outcome is not fixed

- Actions influence future states

In practice: RL is used to train industrial robots to find the most efficient path or adjust their force when assembling delicate parts. Over time, they learn to make fewer errors and complete tasks faster.

6. Digital Twins

A **digital twin** is a virtual representation of a physical system, fed by real-time sensor data. It allows manufacturers to simulate what's happening on the shop floor—or what *might* happen under different conditions.

- Test changes before applying them physically

- Predict performance degradation

- Compare output vs. design tolerances

Digital twins are powered by AI to make simulations dynamic. They can run predictive scenarios, suggest optimizations, or flag potential failures before they occur.

Bringing It All Together

While each of the technologies above can function independently, their real power comes when they are integrated.

Imagine this: A smart factory has a digital twin of its entire production line. Computer vision detects a minor defect forming on a part. That data is fed into an ML model, which predicts a potential equipment misalignment. The reinforcement learning-powered robot arm adjusts its motion accordingly. At the same time, the operator gets an alert via a natural language interface explaining what changed and why.

That's not science fiction. It's the reality in some of the world's most advanced facilities today.

Why Definitions Matter

Understanding what AI truly encompasses in manufacturing is essential—not just for engineers, but for leaders, planners, and policymakers. Too often, AI is seen as a magic bullet. But when broken down into its constituent parts, it becomes clear: AI is a set of tools. When wielded thoughtfully, these tools enable precision, insight, and autonomy on a scale previously unimaginable.

In the next section, we'll explore *why now* is the perfect time for AI adoption—what has changed, what's driving the surge, and why manufacturers of all sizes must act before they fall behind.

1.3 Ten Converging Drivers of AI Adoption

The rise of artificial intelligence in manufacturing is not an isolated phenomenon. It is the result of powerful, overlapping trends that have reached critical mass. Just as the invention of electricity would not have revolutionized factories without the parallel development of motors, transmission systems, and light bulbs, the success of AI today is made possible by multiple enabling forces that are coming together simultaneously.

Let's examine the ten most significant drivers that are accelerating AI adoption across the manufacturing landscape:

1. Data Proliferation

Modern factories generate an unprecedented volume of data. From programmable controllers and machine sensors to quality scanners, ERP systems, and supply chain software, manufacturers are drowning in data—but starving for insights.

Every second, thousands of signals are emitted from production lines: temperature, pressure, flow rate, torque, cycle times, vibration, downtime events, rejection rates, and more. Until recently, most of this data was siloed, underused, or ignored.

AI thrives in data-rich environments. Machine learning algorithms can ingest terabytes of information, identify patterns, and generate predictive insights. What was once just "noise" becomes fuel for optimization, anomaly detection, and decision support.

Example: A packaging plant uses AI to analyze conveyor belt sensor data across 30 machines. By identifying subtle changes in vibration patterns, the system predicts belt misalignments 72 hours before failure—eliminating unplanned downtime.

2. Affordable and Scalable Computing Power

In the past, training complex AI models required prohibitively expensive hardware. Today, advances in cloud computing, edge computing, and GPU acceleration have made this processing power accessible to almost any manufacturer—regardless of size.

With services from providers like AWS, Microsoft Azure, and Google Cloud, even small factories can train models, simulate production scenarios, and deploy AI without purchasing or managing their own data centers.

Edge computing—processing data near the source rather than sending it to the cloud—enables real-time decisions on the shop floor with minimal latency. This is especially important for time-sensitive tasks like robotic movement, machine safety, or instant defect rejection.

3. Cheaper, Smarter Sensors and IoT Integration

Sensor technology has evolved rapidly. Devices that once cost thousands of dollars are now available for a fraction of the price—with better precision, wireless connectivity, and battery life.

With the **Industrial Internet of Things (IIoT)**, manufacturers can outfit legacy equipment with sensors to monitor performance, usage, and environment. These connected devices form the backbone of AI systems, supplying the real-time data necessary for intelligent decision-making.

Example: A legacy injection molding machine, previously operated manually, is retrofitted with thermal, acoustic, and pressure sensors. The data is fed into an AI model that learns the optimal parameter settings for different polymer grades, reducing scrap by 28%.

4. Shorter Product Lifecycles and Demand for Customization

Gone are the days when products remained unchanged for a decade. Today's consumers expect regular updates, new features, and even personalized products.

This means that manufacturing lines must be far more flexible. AI enables dynamic reconfiguration, adaptive scheduling, and design-aware automation—making it feasible to produce small batches or one-off units efficiently.

Example: An apparel manufacturer uses AI to switch printing and stitching operations based on online customer orders. It adapts production runs every few hours without halting operations.

5. Labor Shortages and Skill Gaps

Globally, manufacturing is facing a labor crisis. As experienced technicians retire, fewer young workers are entering the trade. In some regions, more than 40% of skilled positions go unfilled.

AI helps mitigate this by automating repetitive, dangerous, or highly technical tasks. It also assists human workers with decision-making tools, intuitive interfaces, and augmented reality overlays.

Rather than replacing jobs, AI is changing their nature—moving workers up the value chain.

6. Increasing Supply Chain Complexity and Risk

Recent global disruptions—pandemics, wars, port closures, and trade tensions—have exposed the fragility of traditional supply chains.

AI helps by:

- Predicting supplier delays based on historical and live data

- Recommending alternate sourcing in real time

- Optimizing inventory and transportation routes

Example: A multinational electronics firm uses AI to simulate thousands of supply chain scenarios. When a supplier in Taiwan halts production due to a typhoon, the system autonomously reroutes sourcing to a backup in Vietnam, adjusting delivery timelines and procurement budgets instantly.

7. Rising Pressure for Energy Efficiency and Sustainability

Sustainability is no longer optional—it's a regulatory, financial, and ethical imperative. Customers, investors, and governments demand transparency on emissions, water use, and waste.

AI models help manufacturers:

- Monitor energy use per batch or product line

- Optimize HVAC, lighting, and equipment load profiles

- Predict carbon footprint for each SKU

Example: A glass plant uses AI to tune furnace temperatures based on ambient humidity and time of day. This reduces energy use by 14% without affecting output quality.

8. Higher Customer Expectations and Hyper-Personalization

From sneakers to smartphones, customers want their products to reflect personal taste, use case, or identity. They expect speed, accuracy, and transparency—while retaining the price advantages of mass production.

AI enables **mass customization** by dynamically adjusting recipes, tolerances, colors, or features on the fly.

Example: A food company uses AI to adjust granola bar ingredients based on real-time allergen input, customer order preferences, and packaging requests. It delivers 100 SKUs a day using just three production lines.

9. Convergence of IT and OT Systems

For decades, manufacturing ran on operational technology (OT): PLCs, SCADA systems, and MES software. Meanwhile, IT focused on business tools like ERP, CRM, and analytics.

AI demands convergence. Real-time data from the shop floor must flow into enterprise systems—and vice versa. This fusion enables end-to-end intelligence across procurement, planning, production, and delivery.

Companies that bridge this divide gain a competitive edge through total visibility and decision automation.

10. Competitive Pressure and the Fear of Being Left Behind

Perhaps the most urgent driver is the growing realization that *not adopting AI is a greater risk than adopting it.*

Early adopters are already realizing:

- 10–30% productivity increases

- 20–40% defect reductions

- Faster time-to-market

- Enhanced customer satisfaction

Lagging competitors are forced to compete on price—or worse, face obsolescence.

The question is no longer "Should we use AI?" but "How fast can we implement it—and where should we begin?"

1.4 Core Applications of AI in the Factory

Artificial Intelligence in manufacturing isn't confined to theoretical research labs or high-tech showrooms. It's already embedded in real-world operations, driving results from predictive analytics to robotic autonomy. This section explores six of the most impactful AI applications currently transforming factory floors across the globe. Each one is not only technologically feasible today—but financially justified, widely scalable, and increasingly indispensable.

1. Predictive Maintenance

The traditional approach: Run-to-failure models or fixed schedules that waste resources or cause unexpected breakdowns.

With AI: Machine learning algorithms continuously analyze sensor data—such as vibration, temperature, and sound—to detect early signs of equipment degradation. These models predict when a component is likely to fail, allowing proactive maintenance at the optimal time.

Example: A precision metal parts manufacturer used AI to monitor CNC spindle vibration. The model predicted failure 72 hours in advance, reducing emergency downtime by 38% and saving over $220,000 in lost productivity per quarter.

Implementation Tip: Start with one asset class. Use historical failure data to train supervised models and deploy low-latency edge AI devices for real-time analysis.

2. Quality Control via Computer Vision

The traditional approach: Human inspectors at inspection stations, limited by fatigue and inconsistency.

With AI: High-resolution cameras paired with deep learning models inspect surfaces, labels, dimensions, and finishes at high speed and precision. Defect detection systems can classify scratches, dents, smudges, and irregularities invisible to the naked eye.

Example: A smartphone assembly plant implemented AI-based vision systems on their final inspection lines. False positives dropped by 57%, and defect detection accuracy rose from 87% (human) to 99.2%.

Implementation Tip: Start with a high-volume product line where visual defects are common. Use labeled images for training and continuously retrain with new data to improve accuracy.

3. Smart Robotics and Cobots

The traditional approach: Industrial robots programmed for repetitive tasks, limited to fixed trajectories and unsafe for human proximity.

With AI: Modern robots learn from demonstrations, adjust in real time, and safely share workspaces with humans. Reinforcement learning allows robots to experiment with different paths or forces to optimize performance.

Example: An electronics manufacturer uses cobots with AI-powered vision and force sensors to insert fragile connectors. They adjust grip strength based on material sensitivity—something that would be impossible in traditional automation.

Implementation Tip: Begin with low-risk assembly tasks or pick-and-place functions. Integrate perception (camera) and proprioception (touch/force sensors) for adaptive control.

4. Digital Twins for Simulation and Optimization

The traditional approach: Physical trial-and-error testing of new configurations or line setups, often requiring expensive downtime.

With AI: A digital twin simulates the entire production system in real time. It uses actual sensor data to model machine behavior, bottlenecks, and flow dynamics. AI engines run predictive scenarios to recommend optimal changes.

Example: A beverage plant created a digital twin of their bottling line. The system simulated 43 layout variations and found a 12% throughput improvement with a minor conveyor reconfiguration—saving $1.4M in annual costs.

Implementation Tip: Start with a digital twin of one cell or line. Integrate with your MES/SCADA data and apply reinforcement learning for real-time adaptive simulations.

5. AI-Driven Supply Chain Planning

The traditional approach: Fixed rules or spreadsheet-based forecasts with poor visibility into downstream changes.

With AI: Forecasting models ingest data from sales trends, weather patterns, vendor performance, geopolitical risk, and social media sentiment to generate demand and supply predictions. AI optimizes inventory levels, reorder points, and transport routes dynamically.

Example: A consumer electronics company deployed AI-based forecasting across 22 markets. Forecast accuracy improved by 34%, stockouts fell by 27%, and working capital tied in excess inventory dropped by $18 million in the first year.

Implementation Tip: Begin by enriching existing ERP data with external data sources. Use ensemble models to combine demand signals and simulate multiple inventory scenarios.

6. Real-Time Process Optimization

The traditional approach: Fixed recipes or process parameters applied uniformly, despite input variability or environmental conditions.

With AI: Algorithms analyze process inputs (e.g., raw material moisture, ambient temperature, energy cost) and adjust control parameters on the fly for each batch or cycle.

Example: A plastics extrusion facility uses AI to optimize die temperatures based on polymer grade and ambient humidity. This reduced warping defects by 41% and cut energy consumption by 11%.

Implementation Tip: Deploy AI first in energy-intensive or variable-yield processes. Use online optimization tools integrated with programmable logic controllers (PLCs) to auto-tune settings.

The Bottom Line

These six use cases represent the low-hanging fruit of AI in the factory—accessible, practical, and proven to deliver strong ROI. While each stands alone, their combined impact can be exponential. For example, an AI system might predict an upcoming failure (predictive maintenance), adjust robotic workloads accordingly (smart robotics), simulate line changes via a digital twin, and reallocate inventory based on new production output (supply chain optimization)—all autonomously, and in real time.

The future factory isn't built on any single AI application. It is an ecosystem—interconnected, intelligent, and increasingly autonomous.

Up next, we'll explore the measurable financial and operational value that AI brings to manufacturing, along with benchmarking examples and performance metrics.

1.5 Measuring the Value: Quantified Gains

One of the most compelling arguments for AI in manufacturing is its ability to deliver **tangible, measurable value**. In an industry where every second of downtime, every rejected part, and every inefficient energy cycle translates directly to lost revenue, the impact of AI can be seen not just in innovation—but in numbers.

AI is not simply a "nice-to-have" anymore. It is a performance multiplier.

This section outlines the key areas where manufacturers have realized gains by adopting AI and presents real-world performance benchmarks that validate the investment.

Downtime Reduction through Predictive Maintenance

Downtime is one of the most costly events in manufacturing. Whether it's planned or unplanned, it halts throughput, disrupts scheduling, and impacts labor and logistics.

With AI: Predictive maintenance systems forecast failures days—or even weeks—in advance. Instead of replacing components too early or waiting for breakdowns, AI optimizes intervention timing based on actual machine behavior.

Case Example:
 A global automotive parts supplier implemented an AI-powered predictive maintenance solution across 18 CNC machines. Over 12 months:

- Unplanned downtime was reduced by 47%

- Tooling costs dropped by 22%

- Annualized savings: $1.3 million

- Maintenance planning accuracy improved from 62% to 91%

Scrap Reduction and Quality Yield Improvement

Product defects cost manufacturers billions annually—in rework, returns, warranty claims, and brand damage. Many defects arise from process variation, human error, or micro-level anomalies invisible to traditional quality checks.

With AI: Computer vision and ML-based defect detection increase precision, consistency, and traceability. More importantly, AI can trace defects back to specific causes (e.g., operator, machine, material batch) and recommend changes to prevent recurrence.

Case Example:
A packaging manufacturer applied deep learning to its line inspection cameras.

- False negatives dropped from 9% to under 1%

- Scrap rate reduced by 36%

- Root cause analysis time went from 4 hours to 12 minutes

- ROI achieved in 9 months

Throughput and Line Balancing Optimization

Manufacturers often struggle with balancing lines—overburdening one cell while underutilizing others, leading to bottlenecks or idle capacity.

With AI: Real-time data from PLCs, machine vision, and WIP sensors feeds reinforcement learning models that dynamically adjust cycle time, buffer levels, and routing logic.

Case Example:
A consumer goods company used AI to optimize its bottling line. Results included:

- 17% increase in line throughput

- 13% reduction in changeover times

- OEE (Overall Equipment Effectiveness) improved from 68% to 81%

- Avoided $6M in planned capital expenditure for additional lines

Energy Cost Savings and Sustainability Gains

Industrial plants are among the largest consumers of electricity and gas. Traditional methods rely on static energy schedules or reactive controls that waste energy during off-peak operations.

With AI: Models learn patterns of energy consumption and adjust HVAC, compressors, furnaces, and chillers dynamically based on actual load, ambient conditions, and peak tariff windows.

Case Example:
 A steel rolling mill used AI to optimize reheating furnace settings based on order schedules, steel grades, and ambient temperatures.

- 22% energy savings per metric ton

- Carbon emissions reduced by 14%

- Energy cost savings of $3.9M in the first year

Inventory, Logistics, and Working Capital Improvements

Inventory mismanagement ties up cash, fills warehouses, and results in costly shortages or write-downs. AI brings intelligence to demand forecasting, procurement scheduling, and inventory optimization.

With AI: Forecast accuracy improves. Buffer stock can be reduced. Replenishment cycles become demand-driven rather than time-based.

Case Example:
A global electronics manufacturer implemented AI-powered inventory planning across 3 continents.

- Forecast accuracy improved from 71% to 89%

- Working capital tied in excess stock reduced by $14.7M

- Customer fill rate rose from 93% to 98.6%

- Forecasting team headcount reduced by 20% through automation

Labor Efficiency and Workforce Enablement

While AI often raises concerns about job loss, its more common role is **augmentation**—freeing up human effort from routine tasks and enabling focus on complex problem-solving or cross-functional roles.

With AI: Operators receive recommendations, alerts, and visual guidance. Engineers spend less time on manual tuning and more on process innovation.

Case Example:
A specialty chemicals company implemented AI advisors in their control room:

- Reduced operator decision fatigue by 47%

- Training time for new operators dropped from 16 weeks to 8

- Incident resolution time fell by 36%

- Internal survey: 92% of operators preferred working with AI tools over legacy dashboards

Summary: High-Impact KPIs

KPI	Without AI	With AI
Downtime	Frequent, reactive	30–50% reduction
Scrap Rate	8–12%	2–5%
Energy Cost per Unit	Unoptimized	10–25% reduction
Forecast Accuracy	60–75%	85–95%
Changeover Time	Manual	15–35% faster
Operator Efficiency	Variable	Higher consistency, fewer errors

Making the ROI Case

Most AI initiatives in manufacturing can break even within **6 to 18 months**. The key is to start with high-impact use cases that affect critical cost centers or customer KPIs. The best implementations are not those with the most complex models—but those with the clearest alignment between data, decision-making, and business value.

1.6 Sector-Specific Examples of AI in Action

While AI in manufacturing is often discussed in broad terms, its real impact becomes clear when we zoom in on specific sectors. Each industry has unique challenges—tight tolerances, hazardous materials, compliance burdens, global supply networks—and AI is being adapted to address these needs with precision and scale.

Let's explore how AI is transforming four of the most technologically advanced manufacturing sectors today.

Automotive Industry

Overview:
The automotive sector has been a historical leader in industrial innovation—from assembly lines to just-in-time production. But the shift toward electric vehicles (EVs), autonomous systems, and hyper-personalized consumer demand has made AI an operational necessity.

AI Applications:

- **Computer Vision for Assembly Verification:** Cameras inspect welds, paint finishes, part alignment, and cable routing in real time, flagging defects before they leave the line.

- **AI-Powered AGVs (Automated Guided Vehicles):** Self-navigating units optimize parts delivery to specific workstations based on live production scheduling.

- **Demand Forecasting and Inventory Optimization:** AI models analyze dealership sales, market trends, and weather data to forecast spare parts demand with >90% accuracy.

- **Voice-Guided Maintenance Assistants:** NLP systems assist technicians in diagnostics and repair using real-time voice interaction and visual overlays.

Example:
BMW uses AI across 31 manufacturing sites to optimize image recognition, detect tool wear, and fine-tune injection molding machines—resulting in significant scrap reduction and faster cycle times.

Unique Benefits:

- Lower defect rates

- Smarter labor deployment

- Real-time material flow

- Personalized production capability (e.g., trim, infotainment, safety packages)

Aerospace and Defense

Overview:
Aerospace manufacturing deals with ultra-high precision, rigorous safety standards, and complex, low-volume production. The margin for error is zero, and traceability is essential.

AI Applications:

- **Digital Twins for Engine Components:** AI models simulate stress, thermal load, and material fatigue, improving design and reducing prototype cycles.

- **Anomaly Detection in Composites:** Deep learning models inspect carbon-fiber layups and bonded surfaces using high-frequency thermal or ultrasonic imaging.

- **Additive Manufacturing Optimization:** AI tunes 3D printing parameters (laser speed, powder density, layer cooling) to prevent microstructural defects.

- **Supply Chain Risk Mapping:** AI assesses geopolitical, transport, and compliance risks across tiered suppliers to minimize disruptions.

Example:

GE Aviation created digital twins of over 100,000 jet engines in operation. These models predict part replacement needs, improving safety and extending engine life.

Unique Benefits:

- Reduced inspection times

- Lower rework rates

- Accelerated design-to-flight cycles

- Enhanced traceability for compliance (e.g., FAA, EASA)

Pharmaceutical Manufacturing

Overview:
Pharma manufacturing operates in a highly regulated environment. Accuracy, cleanliness, traceability, and process consistency are non-negotiable. Batch failures can cost millions and risk lives.

AI Applications:

- **AI-Based Process Analytical Technology (PAT):** Monitors chemical reactions and adjusts variables in real time to ensure product consistency.

- **Intelligent Scheduling:** AI factors in equipment availability, cleaning validation status, and product compatibility to optimize production sequencing.

- **Defect Detection in Blister Packaging:** Vision systems check foil seals, fill levels, and expiration dates, reducing patient risk.

- **Regulatory Document Automation:** NLP is used to extract and validate compliance data across production records and batch reports.

Example:

Pfizer implemented AI-powered digital twins in vaccine manufacturing during COVID-19. This enabled faster validation cycles, precise scale-up, and adaptive scheduling—reducing ramp-up time by 50%.

Unique Benefits:

- Real-time process control

- Lower risk of batch rejection

- Faster tech transfer between sites

- Enhanced compliance with 21 CFR Part 11 and GMP guidelines

Electronics and Semiconductor Manufacturing

Overview:
This sector requires micro-scale precision, high-speed assembly, and a zero-defect philosophy. With shrinking component sizes and growing complexity, human inspection and manual quality control are no longer viable.

AI Applications:

- **SMT Line Optimization:** AI tunes placement speeds, pick order, and vision alignment for Surface Mount Technology lines.

- **Wafer Inspection:** AI detects lithographic defects at the sub-micron level, often before human technicians can.

- **Real-Time Environmental Control:** Machine learning algorithms control temperature, humidity, and electrostatic discharge conditions in cleanrooms.

- **Chip Design Acceleration:** AI generates and verifies custom logic designs, reducing chip layout time by 30–50%.

Example:
 TSMC uses deep learning models for automatic defect classification in wafers. This has reduced false positives by 40% and allowed real-time corrective action in photolithography.

Unique Benefits:

- Higher throughput in multi-board panels

- Lower false rejections

- Predictive scheduling for maintenance and part binning

- Improved yield per wafer

Key Takeaway

While the tools and techniques of AI may be similar across sectors, their implementation is highly customized. The value of AI lies not just in its core capability—but in how that capability is shaped to fit the domain's constraints, workflows, and objectives.

Aerospace demands precision. Pharma demands compliance. Automotive demands flexibility. Electronics demand speed. AI meets them all.

As we move ahead, the lines between sectors will blur, but one thing is certain: AI is no longer experimental—it's the backbone of next-generation manufacturing across industries.

1.7 Organizational Benefits Beyond the Factory

When most people think of AI in manufacturing, their minds immediately go to robots, sensors, predictive analytics, or automated inspection systems on the shop floor. While these operational applications are indeed powerful, the real potential of AI stretches far wider—touching nearly every function of a modern manufacturing organization.

From R&D and procurement to HR, finance, marketing, and sustainability, AI is enabling faster decisions, higher accuracy, and more strategic alignment across the enterprise.

Let's explore how AI is redefining roles, decisions, and workflows beyond the production line.

1. Research and Development (R&D)

Traditional Model:
R&D has historically relied on trial-and-error experimentation, lab-scale prototyping, and long design cycles. Testing dozens of configurations can take months.

With AI:
AI accelerates the product development cycle by analyzing historical performance, simulating outcomes, and even generating new product designs autonomously.

- **Generative Design:** AI explores thousands of design variations based on constraints like strength, weight, material, or cost.

- **Material Discovery:** Machine learning models identify chemical formulations or composite blends with optimal characteristics.

- **Simulation Modeling:** Digital twins allow engineers to test how a product would perform in the real world—without building a single physical prototype.

Example:

An automotive OEM uses AI to generate lightweight chassis designs, which are then 3D printed and validated—reducing vehicle weight by 17% and prototyping time by 60%.

2. Finance and Cost Control

Traditional Model:
Financial forecasting, budgeting, and cost optimization often depend on spreadsheets and backward-looking reports.

With AI:
AI brings predictive power and real-time insights to financial management.

- **Cost-to-Serve Modeling:** AI calculates the true cost of serving specific customers or product SKUs by analyzing supply chain, labor, and energy usage.

- **Cash Flow Forecasting:** ML models project receivables, payables, and capital requirements with high accuracy.

- **Spend Analysis:** AI classifies and reviews supplier invoices to detect anomalies, identify bundling opportunities, or prevent overbilling.

Example:
A global industrial manufacturer implemented an AI-driven spend intelligence tool. Within 6 months, it identified $3.2M in vendor

consolidation opportunities and $1.1M in
payment term optimizations.

3. Procurement and Supplier Management

Traditional Model:
Procurement relies on supplier scorecards, historical price data, and manual negotiations—often reacting to disruptions rather than anticipating them.

With AI:
Procurement teams use AI to predict price volatility, assess supplier risk, and automate sourcing decisions.

- **Risk Scoring:** AI analyzes news, geopolitical events, credit ratings, and shipping delays to rank supplier stability.

- **Dynamic Pricing Models:** AI predicts raw material pricing and recommends contract adjustments or hedging strategies.

- **Supplier Chatbots:** NLP-powered bots handle RFQs, compliance queries, and documentation exchange autonomously.

Example:
A chemicals company used AI to reroute procurement from two high-risk suppliers before

COVID-19 lockdowns, ensuring continuity and avoiding $7M in production losses.

4. Human Resources and Workforce Planning

Traditional Model:
Hiring, training, and succession planning are often reactive and based on subjective evaluation.

With AI:
AI helps HR teams plan, predict, and manage talent needs more strategically.

- **Skills Gap Analysis:** AI maps current workforce capabilities against future skill demands.

- **Predictive Attrition Models:** Identify at-risk employees and recommend interventions.

- **Smart Recruitment Tools:** Automatically match resumes to job roles and evaluate cultural fit using sentiment and tone analysis.

Example:
A large manufacturing group used AI to forecast reskilling needs based on planned automation projects—developing a proactive training plan that avoided over 180 potential layoffs.

5. Marketing, Sales, and Customer Experience

Traditional Model:
Sales and marketing decisions are based on intuition, past campaigns, or limited segmentation.

With AI:
AI transforms how manufacturers interact with customers—especially in B2B markets.

- **Lead Scoring:** Predict which leads are most likely to convert based on behavior, geography, and purchase history.

- **Product Recommendation Engines:** Suggest relevant products or services based on past orders and similar clients.

- **Customer Sentiment Analysis:** AI scans call transcripts, emails, and surveys to gauge satisfaction and flag churn risks.

Example:
A precision tooling firm integrated AI into its CRM platform. The system flagged upsell opportunities at key accounts based on machine

utilization data, boosting average deal size by 22%.

6. Compliance, Legal, and Document Management

Traditional Model:
Compliance teams manually review contracts, safety documents, and audit trails—slow, error-prone, and labor-intensive.

With AI:
AI automates and enhances legal and compliance workflows:

- **Contract Review Engines:** Identify risky clauses, expired obligations, and missing signatures.

- **Regulatory Monitoring:** Automatically track changes to environmental or export regulations and flag relevant SKUs or plants.

- **E-Discovery Tools:** AI scans thousands of documents to extract facts, timeline evidence, or legal arguments.

Example:
A global aerospace supplier reduced contract review time by 64% using NLP-powered legal assistants trained on industry-specific terminology.

7. Corporate Sustainability and ESG Strategy

Traditional Model:
Sustainability was often an afterthought—tracked in separate reports with little integration into core operations.

With AI:
Sustainability becomes a measurable, optimized, and reportable performance metric.

- **Carbon Accounting Engines:** Track emissions at the SKU, site, or batch level using live energy and transport data.

- **Waste Reduction Models:** Analyze scrap, returns, and packaging to suggest circular economy strategies.

- **Green Supplier Analytics:** Score suppliers on emissions, water use, labor practices, and governance.

Example:
An electronics company used AI to simulate the carbon impact of packaging designs. The system recommended a design that cut emissions by 18% and reduced material cost by 11%.

The New Intelligent Enterprise

The modern manufacturer is not simply a production powerhouse—it is a **data-driven, AI-augmented enterprise**. When AI is integrated across departments, it creates a feedback loop of insight, action, and innovation.

Every decision becomes smarter. Every process becomes leaner. Every role becomes more strategic.

This is not just the future—it's the new standard.

1.8 Overcoming Resistance and Change Management for AI

For all the technical promise of artificial intelligence, the biggest barriers to adoption are not technological—they are human.

Across industries and regions, countless AI initiatives have stumbled or stalled not because the algorithms failed, but because the people using, managing, or impacted by them weren't ready, engaged, or supported. Data may drive decisions, but people drive change.

This section explores the real reasons why employees resist AI, how organizations can manage the transition effectively, and what it takes to turn skepticism into empowerment.

Understanding the Roots of Resistance

To address resistance, we must first understand it. Fear of AI typically stems from a mix of practical, emotional, and cultural concerns:

1. **Fear of Job Loss:** The most common fear is that AI will replace human workers, leading to unemployment or role devaluation.

2. **Loss of Control:** Operators, engineers, and even managers worry they'll lose their autonomy or authority as AI takes over decision-making.

3. **Lack of Understanding:** Many workers see AI as a "black box." Without understanding how it works or what it does, mistrust is inevitable.

4. **Past Tech Failures:** Previous automation or IT projects may have failed or created more work, leading to skepticism of any new digital promise.

5. **Cultural Rigidity:** In some plants, "we've always done it this way" is more than just a saying—it's an operating philosophy.

Common Organizational Missteps

Even with good intentions, many organizations mishandle AI rollouts in ways that deepen resistance:

- **Top-Down Imposition:** Leadership selects and deploys AI tools without involving or educating the users.

- **Lack of Context:** New systems are introduced without clearly explaining the business case or user benefit.

- **Neglecting Training:** Employees are expected to "figure it out" with minimal support or onboarding.

- **Overpromising Results:** AI is sold as a magic bullet, raising unrealistic expectations and subsequent disappointment.

- **Ignoring Feedback:** Real user concerns are dismissed as complaints instead of valuable input.

**A Proven Framework for AI Change
Management**

Successful AI transformation is not just about
model accuracy—it's about organizational
readiness. Below is a 6-part framework for
managing AI adoption that focuses on **people
first**:

1. Communicate the Why

Change begins with purpose. People are more likely to embrace AI when they understand why it matters—to the company and to them personally.

- Explain the strategic drivers (e.g., competitiveness, cost savings, sustainability).

- Share the consequences of inaction (e.g., falling behind peers).

- Emphasize that AI is a tool to help them—not a replacement for them.

Tip: Use storytelling, case studies, and internal champions to bring the vision to life.

2. Involve Users Early

People support what they help create. Bring operators, engineers, analysts, and supervisors into the process from the start.

- Ask them to define pain points that AI might solve.

- Let them co-design dashboards, alerts, and workflows.

- Use pilot programs that demonstrate small, quick wins.

Tip: Involve union reps, shift leaders, or veterans as advocates—they are influencers.

3. Provide Hands-On Training

Nothing replaces hands-on learning. Interactive training builds comfort, capability, and confidence.

- Train in small, focused groups with real data and real problems.

- Use role-specific modules: operator vs. planner vs. manager.

- Repeat sessions regularly, not just once at launch.

Tip: Offer incentives or certifications for completing AI literacy courses.

4. Celebrate Wins Loudly and Often

Positive reinforcement accelerates adoption. Celebrate early wins—even small ones—with fanfare.

- Did AI reduce rework by 8%? Share it in plant meetings.

- Did an operator suggest a tweak that improved results? Recognize them publicly.

- Did a pilot beat forecast expectations? Write a case story and circulate it.

Tip: Convert successes into learning templates for other teams.

5. Be Transparent about Limitations

No AI system is perfect. Be honest about what AI can and cannot do—and where human oversight is critical.

- Share false positives, learning curves, and adaptation periods.

- Set clear thresholds for human override and review.

- Encourage feedback and continual model tuning.

Tip: Create a "bug board" or idea box where users can share observations.

6. Build a Culture of Curiosity, Not Compliance

The most successful AI transformations don't just install systems—they cultivate a culture of experimentation.

- Encourage teams to run their own mini-AI experiments.

- Reward suggestions, even if they don't lead to big savings.

- Train managers to coach, not police, digital adoption.

Tip: Gamify innovation by hosting plant-wide AI challenges.

A Real-World Example

A major automotive supplier in Europe introduced AI for visual defect detection on the paint line. Initial resistance was high—operators feared being replaced, and quality engineers were skeptical of model accuracy.

Instead of forcing deployment, leadership took a step back. They held town halls, invited operators to test the system side-by-side with manual inspection, and incorporated their suggestions into the UI. A floor supervisor was trained as an "AI ambassador" and helped translate tech jargon into day-to-day language.

Within 90 days, the same team that resisted the rollout was now training others. Productivity improved by 11%, false positives dropped by 40%, and morale went up.

The secret? **Ownership.** AI wasn't something done *to* them—it was something done *with* them.

Final Thought

The future of manufacturing isn't just smart—it's inclusive. AI adoption succeeds not when machines outperform humans, but when humans feel empowered by the machines they work with.

AI systems may be intelligent, but only people can make an organization wise. And wisdom is what truly transforms industries.

1.9 Barriers, Risks, and Pitfalls in AI Adoption

While the promise of artificial intelligence in manufacturing is enormous, so are the challenges. Many AI initiatives fail to scale—or fail entirely—not due to technical faults, but because of systemic organizational, cultural, or operational issues.

Understanding the barriers ahead of time helps leaders prepare smarter roadmaps and avoid costly missteps. This section details the most common obstacles, risks, and failure patterns in AI adoption across the manufacturing sector—and how to manage or mitigate them.

1. Poor Data Quality and Fragmentation

AI thrives on good data—but most manufacturing plants have legacy systems with siloed, incomplete, inconsistent, or low-resolution data.

Common issues include:

- Sensor drift or miscalibration

- Inconsistent data labeling or timestamp errors

- Data stored across disconnected systems (MES, ERP, SCADA, spreadsheets)

- Missing contextual metadata (e.g., shift, operator, material batch)

Consequences:
Models built on poor data perform poorly. They may reinforce existing inefficiencies, make inaccurate predictions, or fail to generalize.

Solution:

- Invest in data governance frameworks early.

- Assign data stewards for key sources.

- Conduct data audits before launching any AI initiative.

- Use data cleansing, enrichment, and fusion tools to unify formats.

2. Legacy Equipment and Infrastructure Gaps

Many factories still run on equipment that predates the digital age. These machines lack connectivity, generate no data, or require complex retrofitting.

Challenges include:

- No sensor outputs

- No programmable interface (e.g., PLC)

- High cost of retrofit vs. replacement

- Downtime risk when upgrading older systems

Solution:

- Use edge IoT devices or retrofittable sensor kits (e.g., vibration, acoustic, power meters).

- Focus on pilot lines with modern infrastructure first.

- When upgrading equipment, prioritize digital-readiness alongside mechanical capability.

---

3. Skills Shortage and Talent Mismatch

AI requires a unique mix of skills: data science, domain expertise, systems integration, and change management. Unfortunately, most manufacturers are struggling to find or develop this hybrid talent.

Symptoms of a talent gap:

- Heavy reliance on external consultants

- Disconnected teams (data scientists working without process engineers)

- Low adoption due to poor UI/UX design or training gaps

- Delays due to misunderstood requirements

Solution:

- Create cross-functional teams pairing data experts with plant veterans.

- Launch internal AI academies or digital upskilling tracks.

- Partner with universities and industrial research centers for joint projects.

- Empower "citizen developers" through no-code AI platforms.

4. Organizational Silos and Communication Breakdowns

AI systems often cut across traditional departments—production, maintenance, quality, IT, and logistics. Without cross-functional collaboration, projects get blocked or misaligned.

Examples:

- IT won't approve cloud services required for model deployment.

- Quality refuses to trust AI-driven inspection unless it mimics their current process.

- Operations blocks rollout due to fear of KPI disruption.

Solution:

- Form cross-departmental AI steering committees.

- Define shared KPIs for AI projects (e.g., uptime *and* quality yield).

- Involve end users in model design and interface decisions.

- Communicate wins and setbacks openly to foster shared learning.

5. ROI Uncertainty and "Pilot Purgatory"

Many AI pilots show promise but never scale.
Leaders hesitate to expand projects without
guaranteed ROI, while teams lose motivation
from lack of visible impact.

Why pilots stall:

- KPIs are undefined or unrealistic

- Pilot success does not generalize across
  lines or sites

- Costs of scaling (infrastructure, training,
  support) are underestimated

- Results are not documented in a
  compelling business case

Solution:

- Choose use cases with clear cost drivers
  (e.g., scrap reduction, energy savings).

- Track not only ROI, but time-to-value,
  payback period, and risk reduction.

- Build a scale roadmap from day one: tech, process, people.

- Create internal case studies and champions from successful pilots.

6. Overdependence on "Black Box" Models

Advanced AI models—especially deep learning—can produce highly accurate predictions, but often lack transparency. If users don't understand how the system works, they may distrust or reject it.

Risks include:

- Operators override good recommendations

- Engineers can't troubleshoot model behavior

- Compliance teams block use due to audit risk

Solution:

- Use explainable AI (XAI) techniques to highlight feature importance and reasoning.

- Create visual dashboards that show "why" along with "what."

- Maintain logs of AI decisions for traceability and review.

- Balance model accuracy with interpretability depending on application criticality.

7. Cybersecurity and Data Privacy Concerns

AI increases the digital surface area of a factory—more devices, more connections, more data flows. This invites new risks in a time when ransomware, industrial espionage, and insider threats are on the rise.

Threat vectors include:

- Compromised IoT sensors

- Insecure cloud deployments

- Poor identity and access control

- Leaky APIs between AI systems and MES/ERP layers

Solution:

- Integrate cybersecurity into every AI project's design phase.

- Use zero-trust architecture and encrypted data pipelines.

- Conduct regular penetration testing, especially on edge devices.

- Ensure compliance with standards (e.g., NIST, ISO 27001, GDPR).

8. Vendor Lock-In and Lack of Portability

Many AI tools are proprietary or "black-box" platforms. Once adopted, it becomes difficult to switch vendors, extract data, or migrate models.

Problems include:

- Inflexibility in model updates

- High switching costs

- Incompatibility with future systems

Solution:

- Prefer open standards, APIs, and portable model formats (e.g., ONNX).

- Negotiate SLAs that include access to source data and retrain rights.

- Maintain some internal capability to avoid full dependency on external partners.

Final Word: Plan for the Potholes

Adopting AI in manufacturing is like driving a high-performance car through unfamiliar terrain. You may hit bumps. You may stall. But with the right preparation, visibility, and alignment, you'll stay on course—and reach your destination faster than you ever thought possible.

The next section explores how manufacturers are not just surviving the journey—but turning it into a competitive advantage.

1.10 Ethics, Accountability, and Responsible AI in Manufacturing

As artificial intelligence reshapes manufacturing, it brings not only new opportunities—but new responsibilities. AI systems that make decisions affecting safety, quality, employment, and compliance must be held to a higher standard than traditional software tools. With greater intelligence comes a greater need for **ethical oversight, transparent logic, and accountability mechanisms**.

Ethical AI isn't just a theoretical ideal—it's a **business imperative**. Failing to consider fairness, transparency, or bias can lead to real-world consequences: product recalls, safety violations, legal liabilities, regulatory scrutiny, and loss of stakeholder trust.

This section outlines the core principles of responsible AI in the industrial context, key risks to watch for, and how manufacturers can build ethical frameworks from the ground up.

1. Fairness and Bias in Industrial AI

AI systems learn from data. If that data reflects historical bias, flawed assumptions, or unbalanced samples, the model will **amplify** those distortions. In manufacturing, this may not always look like social bias—but it can manifest as systemic process bias.

Examples:

- A quality inspection model trained only on first-shift data performs poorly on night-shift production, wrongly rejecting good parts.

- A predictive maintenance system prioritizes high-end machinery and ignores smaller equipment, even though both are critical to uptime.

- A supplier score model ranks smaller, diverse-owned suppliers lower because it's biased toward large corporate metrics.

Solutions:

- Use diverse and balanced training datasets.

- Include data from multiple shifts, operators, materials, and scenarios.

- Regularly audit models for performance across subgroups (e.g., lines, locations, vendors).

- Involve cross-functional teams in labeling and validation.

2. Transparency and Explainability

Manufacturing runs on trust—between machines, workers, supervisors, and systems. When an AI system flags a batch for rejection or recommends shutting down a press, stakeholders need to understand *why*.

The danger of black-box AI:

- Operators may override AI guidance out of mistrust.

- Managers may reject AI decisions that contradict past experience.

- Auditors or regulators may require documented rationale behind automated actions.

Solutions:

- Use explainable AI (XAI) tools to show which input features influenced a decision.

- Display confidence scores, ranked factors, and alternative outcomes.

- Provide natural language summaries where appropriate (e.g., "Defect due to rising temperature and RPM drift").

- Create dashboards that visualize model decision paths clearly.

3. Human-in-the-Loop Design

Autonomous AI is powerful—but not always appropriate. Critical systems (safety, compliance, ethics) should involve a **human-in-the-loop** approach.

When to involve humans:

- Decisions affecting product release or rejection

- Safety-critical operations (e.g., robotics, chemical mixing, high-voltage equipment)

- Supplier blacklisting or payment holds

- Employee performance assessment

Implementation:

- Build escalation paths where AI flags exceptions, but humans approve actions.

- Allow operators to provide feedback that influences model tuning.

- Maintain manual override controls that are easy to access and track.

- Log every AI-driven recommendation and human decision for transparency.

4. Accountability and Liability

When an AI system causes a costly mistake—who's responsible? The developer? The data team? The vendor? The plant manager?

Risks include:

- An AI-driven robot damages expensive equipment.

- A misclassified part results in a product recall.

- A model inadvertently discriminates against a supplier or location.

- A safety incident occurs based on an AI-controlled process.

Best Practices:

- Assign clear ownership for each AI system (data, model, outcomes).

- Include AI governance in corporate risk management frameworks.

- Require vendors to disclose how their models were trained and validated.

- Conduct failure mode analysis for AI decisions—just like you would for hardware.

5. Regulatory Compliance and Industry Standards

Manufacturers operate in highly regulated environments. AI systems must comply with industry and national laws—including privacy, safety, labor, environmental, and trade regulations.

Emerging standards and frameworks:

- **ISO/IEC 42001** – The first official standard for AI Management Systems

- **NIST AI Risk Management Framework (USA)**

- **EU AI Act** – Classifies AI systems by risk and mandates transparency, monitoring, and redress

- **IEEE 7000** – Ethical considerations in system design

- **FDA (USA)** – Guidelines for AI in medical device manufacturing and diagnostics

What to do:

- Stay informed on regional regulations impacting AI usage.

- Include compliance teams in AI project reviews.

- Document model behavior, changes, and data lineage for audit readiness.

- Build AI ethics reviews into your product development lifecycle.

6. Privacy and Employee Monitoring

AI systems often monitor not just machines, but people—tracking performance, behavior, and communication. While this can improve productivity and safety, it also raises **privacy and dignity concerns**.

Risks:

- Excessive surveillance leading to employee stress or union disputes

- Implicit bias in monitoring behavior of specific teams

- Lack of consent or awareness about monitoring tools

Guidelines:

- Be transparent about what is tracked and why.

- Anonymize data where possible.

- Use aggregate metrics instead of individual surveillance when feasible.

- Include employee reps in tool design and rollout.

Building a Responsible AI Culture

Ethical AI is not just a checklist—it's a culture. A truly responsible manufacturing organization will:

- Educate everyone on what AI is—and isn't

- Encourage open discussions about trade-offs and risks

- Reward teams for raising red flags or improving fairness

- Integrate ethics into AI design, not as an afterthought but as a first principle

Quote to Remember:

> "Responsible AI isn't about slowing down innovation—it's about sustaining it."

By embedding accountability, fairness, and transparency into every phase of AI design and deployment, manufacturers not only protect themselves—they build systems that are more trustworthy, effective, and scalable in the long term.

1.11 Global Landscape of AI Adoption in Manufacturing

The journey toward intelligent manufacturing is not happening in a vacuum—and certainly not at a uniform pace. Around the world, countries and regions are pursuing AI in manufacturing with different strategies, speeds, and priorities. These differences are shaped by national policies, industrial strengths, labor markets, investment levels, and cultural attitudes toward automation.

Understanding the global landscape gives manufacturers insight into competitive trends, partnership opportunities, and regional threats. In this section, we examine the leading geographies and how their approaches to AI are shaping the new industrial frontier.

1. Germany: The Engine of Industrie 4.0

Overview:

Germany is widely regarded as the intellectual birthplace of the Industry 4.0 concept. With its strong base in precision engineering, automotive, and industrial equipment, Germany has led the push toward smart, cyber-physical production systems.

Key Focus Areas:

- Cyber-physical systems

- Digital twins in discrete manufacturing

- Secure data exchange via the Industry 4.0 Platform

- Government funding for AI research and training

- AI-driven automation in small and medium-sized enterprises (SMEs)

Initiatives:

- *Plattform Industrie 4.0* – A national strategy to define standards and frameworks for smart manufacturing

- *KI-Made in Germany* – A federal AI strategy investing €5 billion by 2025 to ensure ethical and sovereign AI development

- University partnerships with Fraunhofer Institutes and private manufacturers

Competitive Edge:
Germany excels in engineering rigor, standardization, and cross-sector collaboration. Its main challenge lies in scaling digital transformation among mid-sized manufacturers, known as the *Mittelstand*.

2. United States: Private Sector–Led Innovation

Overview:
The U.S. leads in AI research and venture capital investment, thanks to its world-class universities, technology giants, and a thriving startup ecosystem. Unlike other countries, the AI manufacturing drive is largely business-led rather than government-driven.

Key Focus Areas:

- Predictive analytics in aerospace, defense, and energy

- Autonomous robotics and warehouse automation

- Edge computing and cloud-AI hybrid systems

- AI-enhanced additive manufacturing

- AI for maintenance and logistics optimization

Initiatives:

- *Manufacturing USA Institutes* (e.g., MxD, ARM Institute) focus on digital manufacturing R&D

- *NSF AI Institutes* fund university–industry collaborations

- Large-scale pilot programs by Tesla, GE, Boeing, and Caterpillar

Competitive Edge:
The U.S. is strong in horizontal AI platforms and systems integration. However, inconsistent policy frameworks and fragmented SME engagement remain barriers to full-scale AI diffusion.

3. China: Government-Orchestrated Acceleration

Overview:
China views AI as a pillar of its industrial and geopolitical strategy. Backed by long-term national plans and massive funding, China is racing to lead not just in AI research but in **applied industrial AI** across electronics, textiles, heavy industries, and green tech.

Key Focus Areas:

- Computer vision in electronics and textiles

- Real-time scheduling optimization in mega-factories

- AI in battery manufacturing and EV production

- Integration of AI with 5G for real-time control

- AI-based worker productivity systems

Initiatives:

- *Made in China 2025* – A national strategy to move from labor-intensive to tech-intensive manufacturing

- *Next Generation AI Plan* – Includes smart factory pilots in over 100 cities

- AI investments exceeding $70 billion in industrial technology startups

Competitive Edge:
China benefits from data abundance, centralized coordination, rapid deployment cycles, and a culture of digital experimentation. The trade-off: concerns around data privacy and transparency.

4. Japan and South Korea: Robotics-Led Intelligence

Overview:
Japan and South Korea have long dominated robotics and electronics. Their AI strategies focus on augmenting already-automated production systems with intelligence, adaptability, and predictive capabilities.

Key Focus Areas:

- Human-robot collaboration (cobots)

- AI for visual inspection and kanban optimization

- Reinforcement learning in autonomous robotics

- AI-driven energy optimization

- Predictive quality in semiconductor fabs

Initiatives:

- *Society 5.0 (Japan)* – Vision to integrate AI and IoT into everyday life, including manufacturing

- *Korean New Deal* – $160B initiative that includes AI transformation of traditional industry

- AI startup clusters in Osaka, Seoul, and Daejeon

Competitive Edge:
These nations excel in robotic AI, discipline, and long-term planning. Their conservative culture may slow adoption among SMEs, but precision and quality remain world-class.

5. India and Southeast Asia: Leapfrogging Through AI

Overview:
While not historically seen as manufacturing giants, India, Vietnam, Thailand, and Indonesia are emerging as **AI-powered manufacturing hubs**—especially in pharma, electronics, automotive components, and consumer goods.

Key Focus Areas:

- AI in pharma formulation and process control

- Computer vision for garment and apparel inspection

- AI for predictive maintenance in resource-limited settings

- Real-time dashboards for SME operations

- Use of AI in digital worker management and safety compliance

Initiatives:

- *Digital India* and *Make in India* programs with AI skilling components

- Creation of AI Centers of Excellence in cities like Bangalore and Pune

- Public-private partnerships for AI pilot plants in textiles and engineering sectors

Competitive Edge:
These regions offer a combination of low-cost labor, digital-savvy talent, and government support for AI-enabled modernization. Their challenge is scaling infrastructure and upskilling rural or non-English-speaking workforces.

Regional Trends Snapshot

Region	Strengths	Challenges
Germany	Engineering depth, standards	Scaling among SMEs
USA	Innovation and platforms	Fragmented national coordination
China	Scale, speed, state support	Transparency, global trust
Japan/Korea	Robotics, process discipline	Conservative SME adoption
India/SEA	Talent, adaptability, cost	Infrastructure, skill gaps

What This Means for You

No matter where your organization is based, global AI trends affect your competitiveness. Suppliers, customers, and competitors are implementing intelligent systems that could shift:

- Delivery expectations

- Product pricing

- Compliance requirements

- Innovation cycles

To thrive, manufacturers must learn not just from their industry—but from the world.

1.12 Building an AI-Ready Factory: Roadmap and Strategy

Transforming a traditional factory into an intelligent, AI-enabled production ecosystem isn't a matter of plugging in a new tool—it requires vision, preparation, and disciplined execution. While the path will vary by sector, scale, and geography, certain strategic steps are essential for every successful transition.

This section presents a clear, phased roadmap to becoming AI-ready—from initial strategy to full-scale deployment.

Step 1: Define the Vision and Business Case

Every transformation begins with a *why*. AI adoption must be grounded in clear business outcomes—not tech experimentation.

Start by asking:

- What are our top pain points—downtime, yield, rework, demand planning?

- Which KPIs will AI improve—OEE, scrap, cycle time, asset utilization, cost per unit?

- What is our strategic priority—resilience, agility, quality, sustainability?

Key Deliverables:

- Executive-aligned vision statement

- Clear value hypotheses for use cases

- Prioritized pain points mapped to AI potential

Tip: Begin with high-impact, high-feasibility use cases to build momentum.

Step 2: Establish Data and Digital Infrastructure

Data is the raw material of AI—but many plants lack clean, structured, or connected data. Building a solid data foundation is critical.

Tasks:

- Audit available data (MES, ERP, sensors, quality systems)

- Identify gaps, inconsistencies, and silos

- Invest in sensor retrofits, edge devices, and data historians

- Choose platforms for data ingestion, storage, and labeling

Key Technologies:

- IoT gateways

- Data lakes and industrial data platforms (e.g., OSIsoft, ThingWorx)

- Edge computing for real-time inference

- Cloud platforms (AWS, Azure, GCP) for scalability

Tip: Ensure interoperability—your AI system must "talk" to machines, humans, and enterprise systems.

Step 3: Assemble the Right Team

Successful AI initiatives require a mix of skills: domain experts, data scientists, engineers, and business stakeholders.

Roles to consider:

- **AI Product Owner:** Connects business needs with technical execution

- **Data Engineer:** Structures, cleans, and pipelines data

- **Data Scientist:** Designs and trains AI models

- **Process Engineer:** Ensures operational relevance

- **Change Manager:** Facilitates adoption and training

Tip: Keep teams small, cross-functional, and outcome-driven. Empower "citizen developers" through low-code/no-code AI tools.

Step 4: Select and Pilot Use Cases

Not every process needs AI. The goal is to choose focused pilots that deliver measurable value and build internal confidence.

Ideal Pilot Traits:

- Frequent, measurable problem (e.g., tool failure every 3 days)

- Available historical and real-time data

- Clear baseline KPIs for comparison

- High visibility but low operational risk

Common Pilot Areas:

- Predictive maintenance on high-value assets

- Vision-based quality control

- Real-time process optimization

- Inventory demand forecasting

- Energy optimization for furnaces or HVAC systems

Tip: Frame pilots as learning experiments. Even if ROI is unclear, knowledge gained can pay off long-term.

Step 5: Measure, Document, and Learn

After deployment, focus on capturing results and insights—not just ROI, but adoption barriers, training needs, and model behavior.

Metrics to track:

- Operational KPIs (e.g., uptime, yield, energy use)

- Model accuracy and drift

- User adoption rates

- Intervention frequency (manual overrides)

- Feedback from frontline teams

Tip: Document everything—from success factors to surprises. This builds a knowledge base for scaling.

Step 6: Scale with Governance and Flexibility

Once a pilot succeeds, the next challenge is scale: Can the model work across sites, lines, shifts, or products?

Scaling strategies:

- Build a model factory or center of excellence (CoE)

- Create deployment playbooks

- Standardize data structures, ontologies, and APIs

- Implement model monitoring and version control (MLOps)

- Train line managers and operators at each site

Governance Essentials:

- Define model lifecycle policies

- Assign ownership for performance tuning

- Ensure cybersecurity and data privacy compliance

- Align scaled deployments with corporate ESG and financial goals

Tip: Not every use case scales the same way. Customize rollouts by geography, culture, and machine maturity.

Step 7: Embed AI into the Culture

True transformation isn't when AI works—it's when people use it fluently, trust it intuitively, and improve it continuously.

Cultural shifts to foster:

- From "fixing things" to "preventing things"

- From static schedules to dynamic optimization

- From IT-led projects to operations-led innovation

- From dashboards to AI advisors and copilots

Ways to embed AI:

- Gamify AI suggestions and model tuning

- Share success stories across plants

- Launch internal AI innovation challenges

- Recognize employees who improve AI performance

- Build AI training into onboarding and reskilling programs

Tip: AI isn't a tool—it's a teammate. Give it a seat at the table.

The AI-Ready Factory in Practice

When executed well, this roadmap doesn't just change operations—it changes the entire industrial DNA. You move from:

From	To
Reactive problem-solving	Proactive optimization
Siloed decision-making	End-to-end intelligence
Labor-centric diagnostics	AI-augmented insights
Equipment-focused view	Ecosystem-wide visibility
Fixed schedules and logic	Adaptive, self-improving systems

The AI-ready factory is not defined by how much technology it owns, but by how intelligently it learns, adapts, and evolves every single day.

1.13 Looking Ahead: Manufacturing in 2030

The factories of today are already smarter, more connected, and more autonomous than ever before. But if current trends continue—and they are accelerating—then by 2030, we won't just be talking about *automated factories* or *smart machines*.

We'll be living in a world of **intelligent manufacturing ecosystems**, where machines learn continuously, processes adapt instantly, and entire networks operate in harmony, guided not by static schedules but by dynamic AI models.

This isn't a futuristic fantasy—it's a visible, viable trajectory. Let's explore what manufacturing could look like by 2030 and how companies can prepare to lead in that new reality.

1. Hyperpersonalized Production at Scale

Mass production made goods affordable. Mass customization made them personal. By 2030, AI will make **hyperpersonalization** not only possible—but cost-efficient at scale.

Expect:

- Factories capable of switching between SKUs on the fly without downtime

- AI-driven scheduling that adapts to real-time customer orders

- On-demand manufacturing models where lead time drops from weeks to hours

- Virtual product configuration tools connected directly to digital twins

Example:
A customer designs their own furniture piece online. The order is translated into CAD files, optimized via AI for material efficiency, and immediately sent to a smart factory, where robots cut, assemble, and finish the product—shipping it the same day.

2. Autonomous, Self-Healing Systems

By 2030, machines won't just alert technicians when something goes wrong—they'll **prevent failure, correct course, and heal themselves**.

Enablers:

- Edge-based machine learning models

- Real-time condition monitoring and feedback loops

- Actuators that reconfigure motion paths or pressure without human input

- Distributed intelligence across robotic swarms and modular cells

Impact:

- Downtime becomes a rare exception

- Maintenance evolves from scheduled service to AI-led optimization

- Technicians shift from repair to orchestration roles

Quote to Remember:

"Machines won't be just
programmable—they'll be
teachable."

3. Seamless Human–AI Collaboration

Rather than replacing humans, AI will become a **co-worker**—a constant, real-time advisor embedded in every role.

What this looks like:

- Augmented Reality (AR) helmets that show AI-generated instructions during complex tasks

- Voice assistants embedded on the shop floor to answer questions or change settings

- Operator dashboards that *suggest* optimal actions, backed by data

- Skills training delivered by AI tutors based on real-time performance

Outcome:
AI becomes a force multiplier for human talent. A single technician can now supervise, diagnose, and optimize multiple lines using intelligent interfaces.

4. AI-Native Factory Design

Most factories today were built before AI even existed. By 2030, greenfield plants will be **designed around intelligence from day one**.

Features:

- Sensor-embedded walls, floors, and fixtures

- Fully digital infrastructure with 5G+ connectivity

- AI-driven layout design for energy and material efficiency

- Real-time simulation layers for testing changes virtually before physical implementation

Outcome:
Factories evolve like living organisms—able to reshape themselves in response to new market demands or constraints without costly overhauls.

5. Sustainable and Circular by Default

AI will power **sustainability not as a compliance checkbox—but as an economic driver.**

Capabilities:

- Carbon emissions tracked per product, per batch

- AI optimizing for lowest energy, not just highest speed

- Predictive modeling for waste recovery and reuse

- Circular supply chains where offcuts become inputs elsewhere

Example:
A footwear plant uses AI to design shoe soles from recycled materials, track carbon per unit, and predict end-of-life returns for remanufacturing.

Result:
Sustainability becomes not just ethical—but profitable.

6. Federated Manufacturing Networks

By 2030, manufacturers won't work in isolation. Using AI and cloud platforms, they will become part of **federated, distributed production networks**.

What this means:

- Shared manufacturing resources across regions

- AI broker systems route orders to the best-fit facility in real time

- Microfactories closer to urban centers fulfill niche or local orders

- Blockchain and AI ensure transparency across every step of production

Analogy:
Just as cloud computing replaced physical servers with on-demand capacity, **cloud manufacturing** will replace fixed-line production with flexible, location-agnostic fulfillment.

Preparing for 2030: What to Do Today

To stay competitive in the next decade, manufacturers must begin transforming **now**. The journey to 2030 is paved with decisions made in 2025. Here's how to start:

1. **Invest in Infrastructure:** Digitize legacy assets and build unified data platforms.

2. **Embed AI Strategically:** Start small, measure results, and scale.

3. **Upskill Continuously:** Train people not just to use AI—but to improve it.

4. **Design for Agility:** Build systems that can pivot fast—physically and digitally.

5. **Focus on Ethics and Trust:** Ensure transparency, accountability, and fairness are built in.

6. **Partner Broadly:** Collaborate with startups, universities, and global ecosystems.

7. **Think in Systems:** Don't optimize parts—optimize the whole.

Final Thoughts

The future of manufacturing is not automated—it's **autonomous**. Not robotic—but **responsive**. Not rigid—but **resilient**.

In this new era, factories will no longer be static facilities—they'll be living, learning systems. The companies that lead this revolution will be those that understand AI not as a project—but as a **philosophy of continuous improvement**.

Welcome to the world of intelligent manufacturing. The future has already begun.

Conclusion: From Concepts to Commitment

Chapter 1 has laid the foundation for understanding the transformative role of artificial intelligence in manufacturing. We have explored how AI is not just the next step in industrial automation—it is a leap into a new era of cognition, adaptability, and systemic intelligence. From predictive maintenance to autonomous decision-making, from hyperpersonalization to global competitiveness, AI is redefining what it means to design, produce, and deliver.

But perhaps the most important message is this: **AI is not an experiment—it is a necessity.** The companies that recognize this now, that prepare their infrastructure, their people, and their culture, will not just survive—they will shape the future.

In the chapters to come, we will move from vision to execution—from theory to action. Each chapter will explore a core area of manufacturing where AI delivers measurable, repeatable, and scalable impact.

The intelligent factory is no longer a distant ideal. It is already being built—line by line, model by model, decision by decision.

Let's begin that journey—together.

2.0 Introduction: Maintenance Reimagined

Maintenance has long been viewed as a necessary cost center—something that minimizes disruption but rarely adds strategic value. Traditionally, manufacturers have relied on reactive or preventive approaches: fix machines after they fail or replace parts on a schedule, regardless of actual wear. Both strategies have drawbacks—unexpected downtime on one end, unnecessary costs on the other.

Enter AI-powered predictive maintenance.

In this chapter, we explore how artificial intelligence, machine learning, and IoT sensors are transforming maintenance from a reactive burden into a proactive advantage. We'll walk through the technologies, data strategies, deployment models, case studies, and cultural shifts that make predictive maintenance not only possible—but profitable.

2.1 Maintenance Maturity Models

Understanding predictive maintenance begins with recognizing the spectrum of maintenance strategies:

1. **Reactive Maintenance (Run to Failure):** Fix machines when they break. High risk, high cost.

2. **Preventive Maintenance (Scheduled):** Replace or service parts at fixed intervals. Reduces surprises but can waste resources.

3. **Condition-Based Maintenance:** Intervene based on real-time condition (e.g., vibration, temperature). Requires sensors and manual interpretation.

4. **Predictive Maintenance (AI-Driven):** Forecast failures before they occur using historical and live data. Optimize timing, cost, and availability.

5. **Prescriptive Maintenance:** Goes one step further—recommending not only *when* to act, but *how*, *why*, and *what* the impact will be.

2.2 Key Technologies Behind Predictive Maintenance

Predictive maintenance is powered by a stack of technologies that work together to transform raw signals into intelligent decisions.

1. IoT Sensors

- Measure vibration, temperature, pressure, current, acoustics, humidity, and more.

- Provide high-frequency data that reflects machine health in real time.

2. Edge Computing

- Processes data close to the machine to minimize latency.

- Filters, compresses, and analyzes data before sending it to the cloud.

3. Cloud Platforms

- Store historical and real-time data.

- Run machine learning models at scale.

4. Machine Learning Algorithms

- Anomaly detection: Spot deviations from normal behavior.

- Regression models: Predict time-to-failure.

- Classification models: Label failure types and recommend actions.

5. Digital Twins

- Simulate the behavior of assets under different conditions.

- Enable stress-testing and prediction without physical risk.

2.3 Building an Effective Predictive Maintenance Model

To develop a predictive maintenance solution, follow these core steps:

1. Define the Use Case

- What asset(s) will be monitored?

- What failures do you want to predict?

- What is the business impact (cost of downtime, safety, etc.)?

2. Instrument the Asset

- Identify available sensors or install new ones.

- Ensure consistent timestamping and synchronization.

3. Collect and Prepare Data

- Merge operational data (speed, load) with sensor data.

- Label past failure events to create ground truth.

- Engineer features such as rolling averages, FFTs, or wavelets.

4. Train the Model

- Choose model type (e.g., Random Forest, LSTM, Autoencoder).

- Split into training/testing sets and evaluate with appropriate metrics.

5. Validate and Deploy

- Run in shadow mode before full deployment.

- Use thresholds to trigger alerts.

- Tune model periodically based on feedback.

2.4 ROI of Predictive Maintenance

Predictive maintenance can reduce costs and improve reliability across multiple dimensions:

Impact Area	Traditional Approach	AI-Driven Improvement
Downtime	Reactive shutdowns	20–50% reduction
Spare Parts Inventory	Overstocked to be safe	10–30% reduction
Maintenance Labor	Uniform scheduling	20–40% optimization
Equipment Lifespan	Premature part changes	10–25% extension
Safety Incidents	Sudden breakdowns	Fewer unplanned failures
Productivity	Line stoppages	More reliable throughput

Case Study:

A tier-1 auto supplier implemented predictive analytics on 72 stamping machines. They reduced unplanned downtime by 38%, saved $1.1M in labor and material losses, and extended tool life by 18%.

2.5 Types of Predictive Maintenance Models

Predictive maintenance isn't one-size-fits-all. Choose a model based on data availability and operational needs.

1. Statistical Thresholding

- Use control charts and baselines for early alerts

- Works well for simple processes with stable environments

2. Supervised Learning

- Requires labeled historical failures

- Ideal for common, repeatable failure types

3. Unsupervised Learning

- Detects anomalies without labeled data

- Useful for new assets or rare failure types

4. Deep Learning (LSTM, CNNs)

- Captures complex temporal patterns

- Powerful but requires large datasets and compute power

5. Hybrid Models

- Combine physics-based and data-driven models

- Effective when domain expertise is strong but data is limited

2.6 Common Challenges and Solutions

Challenge	Solution
Incomplete Failure Labels	Use anomaly detection or synthetic data augmentation
Sensor Noise or Drift	Apply filters and recalibration routines
Model Drift Over Time	Schedule retraining and monitor model health
Operator Resistance	Provide interpretable alerts and involve users early
Infrastructure Limitations	Start at the edge, sync with cloud incrementally

2.7 Best Practices for Implementation

1. **Start Small:** Pilot on one critical machine or asset class.

2. **Show Value Quickly:** Target use cases with fast payback (e.g., HVAC, motors).

3. **Close the Loop:** Ensure alerts translate to action—integrate with CMMS or maintenance logs.

4. **Train People, Not Just Models:** Equip technicians with context and trust in the system.

5. **Scale Iteratively:** Expand across lines, then plants, then globally—with local tuning.

2.8 The Human Role in Predictive Maintenance

AI is not replacing technicians—it's empowering them.

- Maintenance engineers become reliability analysts.

- Technicians become AI supervisors.

- Operators become first responders to intelligent alerts.

Invest in **change management**, build champions, and celebrate hybrid human-AI successes.

Conclusion: From Reactive Cost to Predictive Power

Predictive maintenance is one of the clearest examples of AI's value in manufacturing. It turns a liability—unplanned downtime—into a strategic capability: uptime as a service. By shifting from "fix it when it breaks" to "predict and prevent," manufacturers unlock massive efficiency, safety, and quality gains.

But predictive maintenance is not just about tools and models—it's about mindset. It requires data stewardship, workforce engagement, cross-functional collaboration, and continuous learning.

Those who invest today will find themselves not just avoiding breakdowns—but building breakthroughs.

2.0 Introduction: Maintenance Reimagined

Throughout the industrial age, maintenance has been treated as a cost to be minimized, a reactive function tasked with keeping machines running and avoiding disaster. Maintenance crews have long worked in the shadows—only noticed when something went wrong. The philosophy was simple: fix it fast and move on. But in today's fast-paced, hyper-competitive manufacturing environment, this outdated mindset is no longer viable.

The cost of unplanned downtime can be staggering. For a major automotive manufacturer, one minute of stopped production can cost upwards of $20,000. For food processors, a failed chiller can mean the loss of tons of perishable product. Even a brief halt in a high-throughput bottling line can disrupt supply contracts and damage a brand's reputation. More than ever, **machine uptime is not just a technical concern—it's a strategic differentiator**.

Traditionally, manufacturers have relied on two dominant strategies:

- **Reactive Maintenance**, also known as run-to-failure, waits for breakdowns. It's easy to implement but carries enormous risk.

- **Preventive Maintenance** involves scheduled part replacements or checkups. While this reduces surprise failures, it often results in unnecessary labor and early component disposal.

Neither strategy is optimal in today's data-rich, high-precision, just-in-time world. These approaches treat maintenance like a blunt instrument—intervening based on calendars or catastrophic events, not real evidence.

This is where AI steps in.

Predictive maintenance (PdM), enabled by artificial intelligence, machine learning, and industrial IoT (IIoT), marks a paradigm shift. Instead of reacting to problems or applying generic schedules, AI analyzes machine behavior in real time—looking for subtle signals that a failure is likely to occur. These systems learn from history, adapt to patterns, and alert operators *before* trouble starts.

But predictive maintenance is more than just an upgrade—it is a redefinition of what maintenance can be:

- It transforms maintenance from a cost center to a **performance enhancer**.

- It empowers teams with foresight instead of hindsight.

- It reduces waste, enhances safety, and extends the life of critical assets.

AI-driven maintenance isn't a luxury reserved for billion-dollar plants with cutting-edge infrastructure. Thanks to affordable sensors, scalable cloud platforms, and increasingly accessible AI tools, predictive maintenance is becoming democratized. SMEs (Small and Medium-sized Enterprises) can now implement powerful PdM systems that were unthinkable even five years ago.

Moreover, predictive maintenance is often a company's **first successful AI use case**. It's relatively low-risk, highly measurable, and deeply relevant to both operations and finance. It also creates a powerful learning opportunity for cross-functional collaboration between maintenance crews, data teams, and plant managers.

The implications stretch beyond individual machines. Once predictive maintenance is successfully deployed on one critical asset, it paves the way for broader **asset intelligence**—a strategy where the entire factory is optimized around health, performance, and longevity. Combined with digital twins, edge computing, and integrated ERP systems, predictive maintenance becomes the cornerstone of a **self-healing industrial ecosystem**.

This chapter takes a deep dive into that transformation. We'll explore the evolution of maintenance practices, the technology stack powering predictive analytics, model-building strategies, deployment considerations, and real-world success stories. We'll also discuss how to overcome common challenges—from data quality to workforce skepticism.

Whether you're a plant engineer, IT manager, maintenance director, or C-level executive, this chapter aims to equip you with the knowledge and roadmap to move your organization from breakdowns to breakthroughs.

The age of reactive repair is over. The future of manufacturing belongs to those who can **predict, prevent, and perform.**

2.1 Maintenance Maturity Models

To understand how predictive maintenance fits into the broader landscape of asset management, it's essential to map out the maturity of maintenance strategies. Manufacturers don't leap into predictive maintenance overnight—they evolve toward it, often passing through multiple levels of technical and cultural readiness.

This progression can be understood through the **Maintenance Maturity Model**—a framework that classifies maintenance approaches into five key stages. Each stage represents a leap not just in technology, but in thinking, resource management, and strategic alignment.

Level 1: Reactive Maintenance (Run to Failure)

This is the starting point for many organizations, especially in older plants or resource-constrained environments. Equipment is operated until it breaks down, and only then is maintenance performed.

Characteristics:

- Minimal planning

- High emergency repair costs

- Frequent production stoppages

- Increased safety and environmental risks

Example:
A hydraulic press motor fails mid-cycle, halting production for four hours while a replacement is sourced. No prior indicators were tracked. Losses include labor, lost output, and expedited shipping fees.

Strategic Outlook:
Often seen in low-volume or highly variable operations where the cost of monitoring exceeds the perceived benefit. However, this approach

becomes untenable in high-throughput environments where uptime is critical.

Level 2: Preventive Maintenance (Scheduled)

Organizations at this stage adopt time-based or usage-based intervals for servicing equipment. Tasks are scheduled based on manufacturer guidelines or historical norms, not real-time data.

Characteristics:

- Maintenance intervals are calendar-driven (e.g., every 500 hours)

- Reduced surprise failures—but at a cost

- Wastes parts with life remaining

- Doesn't catch early anomalies or irregular failures

Example:
A conveyor gearbox is lubricated every three months, whether it needs it or not. Bearings are replaced on schedule—even if still in good condition.

Strategic Outlook:
An improvement over reactive approaches, but can be inefficient. Preventive maintenance often becomes over-maintenance, especially in plants with large numbers of components.

Level 3: Condition-Based Maintenance (CBM)

CBM monitors the actual condition of assets to determine whether maintenance is needed. This typically involves manual or semi-automated data collection (e.g., vibration checks, infrared scans, oil analysis).

Characteristics:

- Maintenance is performed only when needed

- Uses sensor or inspection data as a trigger

- Reduces unnecessary service

- Still relies on thresholds and human interpretation

Example:
A technician performs ultrasound checks on a bearing every two weeks. Spikes in noise levels trigger a scheduled replacement before catastrophic failure.

Strategic Outlook:
CBM represents a major improvement in resource allocation, but still suffers from latency

(data collected only periodically) and subjectivity
(operator-dependent interpretation).

Level 4: Predictive Maintenance (PdM)

This is where artificial intelligence begins to play a central role. PdM uses historical data, real-time sensor feeds, and advanced algorithms to **predict when a failure is likely to occur—before it happens**.

Characteristics:

- Failure is forecasted in advance

- Maintenance windows are optimized

- Reduces downtime, labor, and parts cost

- Requires solid data infrastructure and modeling capability

Example:
AI analyzes vibration and temperature trends on a rotating shaft and predicts a bearing failure in 9 days. The maintenance team receives a task with confidence scores and suggested actions.

Strategic Outlook:
Predictive maintenance transforms maintenance from a reactive task to a proactive business function. It integrates deeply with production scheduling, procurement, and safety systems.

Level 5: Prescriptive Maintenance

Prescriptive maintenance takes prediction a step further. Not only does it forecast failure, but it **recommends exactly what action should be taken, when, and what the impact will be.** It simulates scenarios, quantifies trade-offs, and often initiates autonomous actions.

Characteristics:

- AI generates action plans, not just alerts

- Prescribes maintenance sequences based on cost, safety, and output

- Integrates with ERP, MES, and CMMS systems

- Enables dynamic scheduling and autonomous execution

Example:
An AI model determines that changing a pump seal within 72 hours will avoid a failure that would cost $17,000 in downtime. It automatically generates a maintenance work order and reserves spare parts from inventory.

Strategic Outlook:
Prescriptive maintenance aligns maintenance with broader business objectives—optimizing for financial, environmental, and customer service goals. It represents the pinnacle of asset intelligence.

Choosing Your Path

Not every organization needs to reach Level 5 immediately. What matters is:

- **Knowing where you are**

- **Knowing where you want to be**

- **Creating a roadmap that matches your capabilities, culture, and capital**

This chapter provides not just the technical overview—but the tools to help you ascend this ladder, one intelligent step at a time.

2.2 Key Technologies Behind Predictive Maintenance

Predictive maintenance is not a single technology—it is a **convergence of systems** that collectively turn raw signals into foresight. While the concept of predicting failures has existed for decades, only recent advancements have made it scalable, affordable, and reliable enough for real-world use across diverse manufacturing environments.

This section explores the key technologies powering today's most effective predictive maintenance programs. Understanding how these components interact is essential to designing a system that's accurate, responsive, and sustainable.

1. Industrial IoT Sensors

At the heart of predictive maintenance lies data—and sensors are the eyes and ears of modern assets.

Common sensor types include:

- **Vibration Sensors:** Detect imbalance, misalignment, and bearing issues.

- **Temperature Sensors:** Reveal overheating, friction, or ambient risks.

- **Current and Voltage Sensors:** Monitor electrical anomalies in motors, drives, and circuits.

- **Pressure Sensors:** Identify blockages or system fatigue in pneumatic or hydraulic systems.

- **Acoustic and Ultrasonic Sensors:** Detect leaks, cavitation, or high-frequency anomalies.

- **Oil Quality and Moisture Sensors:** Evaluate fluid health in rotating equipment.

- **Strain Gauges and Load Cells:** Monitor stress, fatigue, and force in mechanical systems.

Modern sensors offer:

- Wireless communication (Bluetooth, LoRaWAN, Zigbee)

- Long battery life or energy harvesting

- Built-in edge computing capability

- Compact, non-invasive form factors

Example:
A motor outfitted with a tri-axial accelerometer detects early-stage bearing defects by analyzing high-frequency resonance. Maintenance is triggered before vibration escalates to failure levels.

2. Edge Computing

Edge computing refers to processing data **at or near the asset**, rather than sending everything to the cloud.

Why it matters:

- Reduces latency—critical for real-time decisions

- Filters and compresses data, minimizing bandwidth use

- Enables local intelligence where connectivity is intermittent

- Supports low-latency anomaly detection and alerts

Devices at the edge include:

- Smart sensors with onboard processing

- Programmable logic controllers (PLCs) with AI extensions

- Industrial PCs with ML inference engines

- Edge gateways that aggregate and relay filtered data

Example:
 An edge device installed on a compressor monitors temperature and pressure at 10Hz. It detects abnormal patterns and instantly triggers a local alarm—without waiting for cloud confirmation.

3. Cloud Platforms

The cloud is essential for **data storage, long-term analytics, model training, and fleet-wide comparisons**.

Cloud capabilities include:

- Scalable storage for years of asset performance logs

- Powerful compute for training complex ML models

- Unified dashboards accessible across sites

- APIs to integrate with ERP, MES, and CMMS systems

- Collaboration between remote teams, vendors, and OEMs

Leading cloud platforms:

- AWS IoT SiteWise and SageMaker

- Microsoft Azure IoT and Machine Learning Studio

- Google Cloud IoT Core and Vertex AI

- Industrial-specific platforms like Siemens MindSphere, GE Predix

Example:
An aerospace supplier uploads data from 400 spindle motors to the cloud. Engineers train a failure classification model using TensorFlow on GPU instances, which is then pushed back to edge devices for deployment.

4. Machine Learning Algorithms

The "intelligence" in predictive maintenance comes from **machine learning (ML)**—systems that learn patterns, detect anomalies, and make forecasts based on data.

Types of ML used:

- **Anomaly Detection:** Flag deviations from expected behavior (Autoencoders, Isolation Forests).

- **Time-Series Forecasting:** Predict future sensor values or degradation trends (ARIMA, LSTM).

- **Failure Classification:** Categorize issues by root cause (Random Forest, SVM).

- **Remaining Useful Life (RUL) Estimation:** Predict time to failure using survival analysis or regression.

Requirements for effective ML:

- High-quality, labeled historical failure data

- Feature engineering (e.g., FFTs, moving averages)

- Synchronized timestamping across sensors

- Continuous retraining to avoid model drift

Example:
A deep learning model trained on 3 years of compressor data identifies early rotor misalignment patterns and predicts failure with 92% accuracy seven days in advance.

5. Digital Twins

A **digital twin** is a virtual replica of a physical asset or process, updated in real time via sensor data.

Uses in maintenance:

- Simulate how equipment responds to different conditions

- Compare expected vs. actual performance

- Run stress scenarios without physical risk

- Visualize potential failures and intervention outcomes

Types of twins:

- **Component-level:** Single asset, like a pump or gearbox

- **System-level:** Line or machine cell

- **Process-level:** End-to-end workflow or facility

Example:
A digital twin of an injection molding machine shows how changes in mold temperature and cycle time affect product quality. The AI model prescribes optimal settings to maximize uptime and reduce defects.

Integration Is the Key

Each of these technologies is powerful alone—but their true strength lies in **integration**. When sensor data flows to edge devices, analyzed by AI, visualized via cloud dashboards, and simulated by digital twins, manufacturers gain not just insight—but actionable intelligence.

In the next section, we'll explore how to build and deploy these models—turning your asset data into forecasts, and your forecasts into results.

2.3 Building an Effective Predictive Maintenance Model

At the core of predictive maintenance lies the predictive model—a machine learning system trained to recognize early signs of failure before they become catastrophic. But building this model isn't just about writing code or deploying an algorithm. It's a **multi-stage process** that requires clean data, domain expertise, iterative development, and cross-functional collaboration.

This section outlines a practical roadmap to building and deploying effective predictive maintenance models that deliver measurable value.

Step 1: Define the Use Case Clearly

Before writing a single line of code, you must define:

- **What problem are we solving?**

- **What equipment is most critical to monitor?**

- **What types of failure are we trying to predict—and what are their business consequences?**

Focus on high-value, high-risk assets first. For example, a single unplanned shutdown of a bottling line or CNC spindle may result in hours of lost production, making it a prime candidate for predictive modeling.

Checklist:

- Asset criticality matrix (impact vs. frequency)

- Business case tied to failure avoidance

- Specific KPIs to track (e.g., MTBF, downtime hours, defect rate)

Step 2: Instrument the Asset

To predict failure, you must first **sense the conditions that lead to it**. That requires selecting and placing the right sensors.

Considerations:

- What parameters correlate with failure (e.g., vibration, heat, pressure)?

- Are sensors already available, or do we need to retrofit?

- Where should sensors be placed to capture meaningful signals?

- How often should data be collected (sampling frequency)?

Best Practices:

- Use tri-axial vibration sensors for rotating equipment

- Monitor both ambient and internal temperatures

- Synchronize sensor readings with PLC or machine cycle data

- Capture baseline "healthy" behavior for comparison

Step 3: Collect and Label Historical Data

AI models require **training data**—examples from the past that teach the model how to distinguish normal behavior from degradation or failure.

What to collect:

- Raw sensor data (time-stamped)

- Machine logs and alarms

- Maintenance history and service tickets

- Operator notes or fault reports

- Environmental and operating condition data

Labeling Tips:

- Identify known failure events and mark them in the dataset

- Segment timelines into "healthy," "warning," and "failed" zones

- Use domain experts to validate event labeling (e.g., vibration spike ≠ failure unless confirmed)

Challenge:
Historical data is often messy. Expect missing values, inconsistent timestamps, and gaps in labeling. Clean and preprocess the data meticulously—it sets the foundation for everything that follows.

Step 4: Engineer Features and Select a Model

Feature engineering transforms raw sensor inputs into meaningful variables the model can learn from.

Examples of engineered features:

- Rolling means and standard deviations

- Fast Fourier Transform (FFT) to extract vibration frequency patterns

- Temperature gradients or rates of change

- Load vs. performance correlations

- Sensor fusion: combining multiple readings to infer complex conditions

Model Types to Consider:

- **Logistic Regression / Decision Trees:** For binary failure classification

- **Random Forest / Gradient Boosting:** For higher accuracy with tabular data

- **Autoencoders / Isolation Forests:** For unsupervised anomaly detection

- **LSTM / GRU Networks:** For time-series sequence modeling

- **Survival Analysis / Cox Regression:** For predicting Remaining Useful Life (RUL)

Model Selection Tips:

- Use simple models for interpretability if plant operators will review output

- Use complex models (e.g., neural networks) when accuracy is paramount and black-box tradeoffs are acceptable

- Always validate models using train/test splits and cross-validation

Step 5: Validate with Metrics That Matter

Choose metrics that reflect both **technical accuracy** and **business value**:

- **Precision/Recall:** Important when false alarms are costly or dangerous

- **AUC-ROC:** For balanced classification assessment

- **RMSE / MAE:** For continuous RUL prediction

- **Lead Time to Failure:** Time between alert and actual event

- **Uptime Improvement / Cost Savings:** Ultimate value KPIs

Validation Tip:
Deploy the model in "shadow mode" first—where it runs live but doesn't trigger actions. Compare its predictions to actual outcomes for several weeks.

Step 6: Deploy and Monitor in Production

Once the model proves its value, it must be embedded into daily operations.

Steps to productionize:

- Connect the model to real-time sensor feeds

- Set alert thresholds or confidence levels

- Build dashboards that show health scores, RUL estimates, and recommendations

- Integrate with your Computerized Maintenance Management System (CMMS) to auto-generate work orders

- Create audit logs for compliance and learning

Model Monitoring:

- Check for model drift (e.g., changing behavior over time)

- Periodically retrain on new data

- Solicit operator feedback to improve model trust and usability

---

Step 7: Continuously Improve

Predictive maintenance is not a "set and forget" project. It evolves over time:

- Add new sensors or data sources

- Refine failure definitions and labeling

- Tune model hyperparameters

- Compare performance across sites or machine models

- Document learnings and best practices for future use cases

Summary

Building a predictive maintenance model is both an art and a science. It requires close collaboration between maintenance experts, data engineers, operators, and business stakeholders. Done well, it doesn't just detect failure—it enables a smarter, more agile manufacturing environment where machines, people, and AI work in harmony.

Up next, we'll quantify the gains predictive maintenance can deliver—turning insight into impact.

2.4 ROI of Predictive Maintenance

One of the strongest arguments for adopting predictive maintenance is its **clear and measurable return on investment (ROI)**. Unlike speculative technologies that promise future benefits, predictive maintenance offers hard savings in real-world terms: reduced downtime, longer asset life, lower labor costs, fewer defects, and less waste.

When properly implemented, predictive maintenance programs often **pay for themselves within 6 to 18 months**. This section outlines the specific areas where value is created and provides real case studies to demonstrate how those savings are realized across multiple industries.

The Six Core Value Streams

1. Reduced Unplanned Downtime

Unplanned equipment failure can cost tens of thousands of dollars per hour—especially in continuous or high-volume manufacturing. Predictive maintenance anticipates failures, allowing interventions to be planned without disrupting production.

- **Impact:** 20–50% reduction in unplanned downtime

- **Example Metric:** Downtime hours per quarter

- **Savings Source:** Preserved throughput, avoided contract penalties, fewer urgent repair costs

Case Study:
A food processing plant saved over $750,000 annually by using AI to predict bearing wear in its refrigeration compressors, reducing spoilage and emergency service calls.

2. Optimized Maintenance Scheduling

Instead of replacing components on fixed schedules (regardless of actual condition), predictive models recommend intervention only when truly needed. This reduces unnecessary part replacement and labor hours.

- **Impact:** 20–40% reduction in planned maintenance tasks

- **Example Metric:** Mean Time Between Maintenance (MTBM)

- **Savings Source:** Deferred labor, reduced parts inventory, extended equipment life

Case Study:
A tire manufacturer extended average motor service intervals from 90 to 130 days after implementing sensor-driven predictive insights—saving $180,000 in labor annually.

3. Inventory and Spare Parts Reduction

Because predictive models provide early alerts, procurement teams can manage parts inventory with confidence. This reduces the need for excessive buffer stock or last-minute rush orders.

- **Impact:** 10–30% reduction in spare part inventory levels

- **Example Metric:** Inventory turnover rate

- **Savings Source:** Lower capital lock-up, reduced spoilage, better warehouse utilization

Case Study:
An aerospace components firm aligned procurement with AI-driven failure forecasts, eliminating $1.4M in redundant stock over two fiscal years.

4. Asset Life Extension

Operating equipment with proactive maintenance reduces stress and avoids cascading failures. AI helps ensure parts are neither overused nor replaced prematurely.

- **Impact:** 10–25% increase in useful life of major assets

- **Example Metric:** Mean Time to Failure (MTTF)

- **Savings Source:** Deferred capital expenditures, lower asset replacement cost

Case Study:
A cement producer extended kiln gear lifespan by 3 years using vibration analysis and predictive modeling—avoiding a $2.8M overhaul.

5. Energy Efficiency and Environmental Impact

Poorly maintained machines often consume more power or produce emissions outside of regulatory bounds. Predictive maintenance ensures optimal performance.

- **Impact:** 5–20% energy savings in motors, chillers, and compressors

- **Example Metric:** kWh per unit output or per runtime hour

- **Savings Source:** Lower energy bills, reduced carbon footprint, ESG compliance

Case Study:
A bottling plant reduced compressed air system energy use by 17% after AI identified early-stage valve leaks and control tuning issues.

6. Safety and Compliance Enhancement

Unplanned failures increase safety risk for operators, especially in high-pressure, high-temperature, or electrically intensive systems. Predictive maintenance improves reliability and reduces emergency interventions.

- **Impact:** Fewer emergency maintenance incidents

- **Example Metric:** Safety incident reports linked to equipment failure

- **Savings Source:** Avoided medical costs, legal exposure, and regulatory penalties

Case Study:
An oil refinery reduced maintenance-related safety incidents by 35% after deploying a predictive alerting system across rotating equipment.

Holistic ROI Model

Here's a simplified model to estimate predictive maintenance ROI over 12 months for a medium-sized facility:

Value Area	Annual Savings Estimate
Reduced Downtime	$500,000
Maintenance Optimization	$150,000
Parts Inventory Savings	$100,000
Energy Efficiency Gains	$70,000
Asset Life Extension	$130,000
Safety & Compliance	$50,000
Total	**$1,000,000+**

Investment:

- Sensors: $200,000

- Software/Cloud: $80,000

- Integration & Labor: $70,000

- **Total: $350,000**

Payback Period: 4.2 months

Beyond ROI: Strategic Benefits

While direct cost savings are compelling, predictive maintenance also delivers **non-financial advantages** that strengthen long-term competitiveness:

- **Improved customer satisfaction** (fewer delays and quality issues)

- **Better employee engagement** (less firefighting, more strategic work)

- **Data maturity** (foundation for other AI initiatives)

- **Agility** (faster response to changing production demands)

- **Regulatory readiness** (proactive compliance documentation)

Summary

Predictive maintenance is one of the few industrial investments that creates value across every major stakeholder group—from CFOs (cost savings), to plant managers (uptime), to operators (safety), to customers (on-time delivery). It provides immediate operational ROI while laying the groundwork for broader digital transformation.

In the next section, we'll examine how predictive maintenance looks in different industries—highlighting variations in sensors, models, and implementation strategies.

2.5 Sector-Specific Models and Examples

While the core principles of predictive maintenance are universal, **its implementation varies dramatically by sector**. Different industries prioritize different metrics, face unique failure modes, and operate within distinct regulatory environments. This section explores how predictive maintenance adapts to these realities across several major sectors, along with real-world examples of success.

---

1. Automotive Manufacturing

Context:
Automotive plants operate high-speed, highly automated production lines where downtime can cost millions per day. Equipment like stamping presses, paint booths, robotics, and conveyors are critical.

Focus Areas:

- Robotic arm joint degradation

- Conveyor motor health

- Spot weld tip wear and cap life

- Paint booth ventilation fan vibration

Tech Stack:

- High-frequency vibration and acoustic sensors

- PLC-integrated AI alerting

- Real-time feedback to MES systems

Example:

A major U.S. auto OEM deployed predictive analytics across 1,200 robots on its assembly line. By identifying early-stage joint misalignment and increased servo torque, the company reduced emergency repairs by 42% and saved $1.9M in annual downtime costs.

2. Food and Beverage

Context:
 F&B manufacturers require ultra-high availability and strict hygienic compliance. A failed chiller, clogged nozzle, or pressure drop can result in spoiled batches and regulatory violations.

Focus Areas:

- Compressors and chillers

- CIP (clean-in-place) system health

- Pump wear and flow inconsistencies

- Packaging line malfunctions

Tech Stack:

- Wireless temperature and pressure sensors

- Real-time microbiological condition monitors

- Cloud AI for energy and process optimization

Example:

A dairy bottling facility integrated AI-powered vibration and pressure sensors on its filling line. The system predicted pump cavitation due to seal wear and prevented three unplanned stops per week, resulting in a 26% increase in line uptime and $480,000 in product recovery per year.

3. Energy and Utilities

Context:
Power plants, wind farms, and utility grids use capital-intensive equipment where failures have large-scale impact. Predictive maintenance can reduce the risk of blackouts, improve safety, and extend asset life.

Focus Areas:

- Turbine blade erosion

- Generator winding degradation

- Substation transformer temperature drift

- Solar inverter performance anomalies

Tech Stack:

- Long-range SCADA integration

- Infrared thermography

- AI-based weather-adjusted asset forecasting

Example:
 A wind farm operator applied machine learning
to SCADA data across 180 turbines. The system
predicted gearbox failures 25 days in advance
with 88% accuracy. As a result, the operator
avoided $6M in repair costs and optimized
maintenance scheduling based on wind
availability.

4. Pharmaceutical Manufacturing

Context:
Pharma manufacturing must comply with strict regulations (e.g., FDA, GMP). Any failure not only causes losses—it can halt production and trigger audits.

Focus Areas:

- Reactor temperature and mixing profiles

- HVAC filter clogging

- Chiller and cleanroom equipment reliability

- Autoclave sensor drift

Tech Stack:

- Cleanroom-rated sensors

- Batch process digital twins

- AI anomaly detection for batch deviation alerts

Example:

A contract pharma manufacturer used AI to monitor thermal degradation in an air handling unit critical to sterile environments. The system detected fan imbalance two weeks before failure, maintaining compliance and avoiding a full batch discard worth over $300,000.

5. Heavy Equipment and Mining

Context:
Remote locations, heavy-duty usage, and harsh conditions make predictive maintenance critical in this sector. Equipment failures often occur far from service centers, making early warnings vital.

Focus Areas:

- Excavator hydraulic pressure

- Dump truck engine performance

- Conveyor belt misalignment

- Crushing mill temperature and motor torque

Tech Stack:

- Ruggedized wireless sensor networks

- Satellite connectivity for remote AI inference

- Edge AI with autonomous drone inspection

Example:

A copper mining operation deployed edge AI for real-time analysis of motor vibration and current in crushers. They predicted belt tension failures that previously went undetected—improving throughput by 19% and extending asset life cycles.

6. Electronics and Semiconductor

Context:
This sector relies on extremely sensitive, precise, and high-throughput equipment. Micro-defects caused by tool wear or contamination can result in mass-scale product rejections.

Focus Areas:

- Wafer stepper lens alignment

- Plasma etch uniformity degradation

- Fan filter unit reliability

- Thermal cycling impact on circuit boards

Tech Stack:

- Sensor fusion with environmental controls

- AI-driven wafer inspection and yield mapping

- RUL (Remaining Useful Life) for etching chambers

Example:
A global semiconductor fab implemented machine learning to forecast etch tool performance drift. Maintenance intervals were adjusted dynamically, resulting in a 15% increase in throughput per tool and a 7% reduction in energy usage.

Summary

While the algorithms and frameworks behind predictive maintenance remain consistent, **its deployment must be tailored to each sector's realities**:

Sector	Unique Factor	Common Failure Risks
Automotive	High automation, cycle rates	Servo wear, robotic drift
Food & Beverage	Hygiene & perishables	Chiller faults, CIP system failures
Energy	Remote assets, environmental stress	Gearbox wear, thermal imbalance
Pharma	Regulatory pressure	HVAC clogging, batch variability

| Heavy Equipment | Harsh environments, logistics | Belt misalignment, hydraulic leaks |
| Electronics | Micro-level defects | Plasma tool degradation, filter drift |

A one-size-fits-all approach to predictive maintenance doesn't work. **Adaptability, not just intelligence, is the true power of AI in maintenance.**

2.6 Common Challenges and Solutions

Despite its potential to transform asset reliability and reduce costs, predictive maintenance is **not a plug-and-play solution**. Many organizations encounter roadblocks that delay implementation or erode confidence in AI-driven systems.

Understanding these barriers ahead of time—and planning strategies to overcome them—is crucial to unlocking the full value of predictive maintenance. This section identifies the most frequent obstacles and provides real-world solutions based on successful industrial deployments.

1. Poor Data Quality or Incomplete Historical Records

The Problem:
Predictive maintenance relies on large volumes of clean, labeled data. However, many plants lack sufficient failure history, sensor coverage, or synchronized timestamping. Data is often fragmented across systems (MES, CMMS, Excel) and lacks contextual metadata like ambient conditions or operator shifts.

The Solution:

- **Start with what you have**—even small datasets can be used for anomaly detection.

- **Implement data normalization and validation rules** to catch outliers and gaps.

- **Use domain knowledge** to fill labeling gaps or approximate failure boundaries.

- **Log new data immediately** using IoT sensors and tag systems.

- **Consider synthetic data** (e.g., simulated degradation via digital twins) to boost model robustness.

Tip: Don't wait for a "perfect" dataset. Start small, model iteratively, and refine over time.

2. Model Accuracy vs. Interpretability

The Problem:
Advanced AI models like neural networks may produce accurate predictions—but they're often "black boxes." Operators and engineers may be reluctant to trust models they don't understand, especially if they suggest interventions on critical machines.

The Solution:

- Use **Explainable AI (XAI)** techniques like SHAP, LIME, or feature importance charts to show how decisions are made.

- Begin with **interpretable models** (e.g., decision trees, logistic regression) where possible, and layer in complexity as trust grows.

- Visualize anomalies or deterioration trends in intuitive dashboards—e.g., heat maps, time series, or risk scores.

- Integrate model output with existing workflows (e.g., CMMS alerts) to build confidence gradually.

Tip: Early buy-in often hinges on trust. Show the "why," not just the "what."

3. Sensor Noise and Environmental Drift

The Problem:
Industrial environments are noisy—both physically and digitally. Sensor readings can be influenced by ambient temperature, vibration from nearby equipment, or even electromagnetic interference. Over time, sensors themselves may drift or degrade.

The Solution:

- Apply **signal conditioning techniques** like smoothing, normalization, and windowing.

- Use **sensor fusion**—combining inputs from multiple sensors to improve reliability.

- Calibrate sensors regularly and track their age in the maintenance system.

- Flag and exclude faulty sensor data from training and inference processes.

- Consider **edge filtering** to preprocess data before it enters cloud models.

Tip: Don't let perfect be the enemy of good. Models can tolerate some noise if it's consistent and managed.

4. Limited Technical Skillsets

The Problem:
Many maintenance teams lack data science experience, and many data scientists lack manufacturing domain knowledge. Without cross-disciplinary collaboration, projects stall or underperform.

The Solution:

- Create **cross-functional teams** including reliability engineers, IT staff, and data scientists.

- Train operators and technicians in AI basics using hands-on labs or vendor resources.

- Leverage **low-code/no-code platforms** for rapid prototyping and deployment.

- Use external consultants for pilot projects—but plan for internal capability-building.

Tip: Treat upskilling as a parallel investment. AI should not remain confined to a specialist silo.

5. Change Resistance from the Frontline

The Problem:
Technicians and line supervisors may resist AI because they feel it threatens their roles or second-guesses their judgment. Past experiences with overhyped tools or "management fads" can create skepticism.

The Solution:

- Involve frontline users early in pilot design and feedback loops.

- Highlight how AI augments—not replaces—their expertise.

- Share success stories and recognize operators who catch or prevent failures based on AI insights.

- Deploy "shadow mode" first to validate model output alongside human decision-making.

Tip: Make AI adoption a source of pride, not fear. Let the tools earn trust by delivering results.

6. Scalability Issues Across Lines or Plants

The Problem:
A model trained on one machine or site may not generalize to others due to differences in operating conditions, equipment age, or process settings.

The Solution:

- Use **transfer learning** to adapt models to new machines without retraining from scratch.

- Maintain **modular architectures** where sensor mappings and thresholds can be site-specific.

- Standardize sensor naming, data schemas, and CMMS integration across plants.

- Document scaling plans during pilot phases, not after success.

Tip: Don't overfit your first model to one environment. Design with reuse in mind.

7. Integration Challenges with Existing Systems

The Problem:
Even accurate AI predictions are useless if they don't trigger action. Without integration into maintenance management systems, alerting tools, or operator dashboards, insights get lost.

The Solution:

- Use **middleware or APIs** to link predictive tools with CMMS, ERP, or MES platforms.

- Automate work order generation based on AI outputs.

- Embed model scores into operator HMIs (Human-Machine Interfaces) for instant visibility.

- Use MQTT, OPC-UA, or REST APIs for real-time interoperability.

Tip: Don't stop at the model—design for decisions.

Summary

Every predictive maintenance journey faces obstacles. What separates successful organizations is not that they avoid challenges—but that they **anticipate, plan for, and learn through them**.

By addressing these hurdles proactively, manufacturers not only improve their AI systems—they improve their culture of continuous improvement and cross-functional collaboration.

In the next section, we'll examine the **human side of predictive maintenance**—how AI transforms roles, enhances skills, and elevates the people behind the machines.

2.7 The Human Role in Predictive Maintenance

One of the most common misconceptions about AI in manufacturing is that it will replace people. While predictive maintenance does reduce manual checks and reactive firefighting, its true value lies in how it **augments human intelligence**—not how it eliminates it.

Predictive maintenance, when implemented effectively, elevates the role of maintenance personnel from **technician to tactician, from repairer to reliability strategist**. It changes not only what people do—but how they see their value in the organization.

From Reactive Repair to Proactive Reliability

In traditional environments, maintenance teams are often in crisis mode—responding to breakdowns, rushing to source parts, and performing late-night interventions under pressure. It's exhausting, repetitive, and limits strategic thinking.

With predictive maintenance:

- **Technicians shift from responding to planning**

- **Time is spent analyzing patterns instead of chasing parts**

- **Effort goes into improving uptime—not just restoring it**

This transition reduces physical strain, improves morale, and enables deeper involvement in continuous improvement initiatives.

New Roles and Skillsets

Predictive maintenance creates opportunities for upskilling and cross-functional growth. As data becomes central to reliability decisions, new hybrid roles emerge:

Traditional Role	AI-Augmented Role
Maintenance Technician	Reliability Analyst
Line Supervisor	Uptime Performance Coordinator
Condition Monitoring Tech	Data-Driven Asset Health Specialist
Plant Engineer	Digital Twin Operator
CMMS Planner	Predictive Work Order Strategist

These roles combine tribal knowledge with digital literacy—turning seasoned hands into strategic advisors.

Decision-Making Becomes Data-Driven

In the past, decisions were often based on gut feel or rough heuristics. ("We always change this belt every 60 days because once it snapped.")

With AI:

- Decisions are backed by **probability, trend analysis, and confidence scores**

- Failure forecasts are visualized, not just assumed

- Work orders are prioritized by **risk-to-output**, not just calendar

This transition can be deeply empowering. Maintenance teams go from defending their budget to **demonstrating their value with metrics**.

Building Trust Between People and AI

Trust is not built overnight—especially when a new system begins to challenge long-held routines. But trust is critical to adoption.

How to build it:

1. **Co-create models with operators:** Let them help define what "normal" and "abnormal" look like.

2. **Validate predictions side-by-side:** Run models in "shadow mode" alongside human judgment.

3. **Close the feedback loop:** Allow technicians to flag false positives or improve model logic.

4. **Celebrate wins:** Recognize when AI-enabled decisions prevent downtime or save costs.

Quote from a plant technician:

> "It's not that I don't trust the AI. I just need to see that it knows what I know—then I'll trust it to know what I don't."

Real-World Impact: Operator Testimony

Before AI:

- Spent 60% of time on unplanned repairs

- Limited visibility into asset condition

- High stress from last-minute crises

After AI-Powered Maintenance:

- Receives weekly health reports with confidence scores

- Plans service proactively during non-peak hours

- Feels ownership over system improvements

Operator Reflection:

"Now I walk into the plant knowing where I'm needed most. I'm not chasing problems—I'm preventing them."

Training and Enablement

The shift to predictive maintenance demands more than technology—it requires **continuous training and cultural adaptation**.

Training should include:

- Understanding how AI models interpret sensor data

- Reading and interpreting risk scores or health indices

- Using dashboards or mobile apps to trigger actions

- Reporting anomalies back to improve model performance

- Change management support for adapting to new workflows

Some companies go further—creating **internal "AI Champions"** among frontline workers who mentor others and help translate digital initiatives into daily routines.

A Culture of Empowerment

Predictive maintenance, at its best, creates a culture where:

- Technicians are seen as strategic assets

- Data is a team tool, not a management weapon

- Decisions are made with foresight, not hindsight

- Ownership of uptime is shared—not assigned

This cultural shift often has a **halo effect** beyond the maintenance department, inspiring other functions (quality, safety, production) to explore intelligent tools and collaborative problem-solving.

Summary

AI does not replace the maintenance workforce—it elevates it.

It frees teams from drudgery and empowers them to contribute to strategic outcomes. It turns the factory floor into a place of **learning, foresight, and pride**—where the value of every human decision is amplified by data and guided by intelligence.

In the final section of this chapter, we'll summarize what it takes to **successfully implement predictive maintenance at scale**, turning isolated pilots into enterprise-wide advantage.

2.8 Scaling Predictive Maintenance Across the Enterprise

A successful pilot in predictive maintenance is an achievement—but scaling that success across the enterprise is the real milestone. Many organizations start strong with isolated projects, only to find themselves stuck in "pilot purgatory," where proof-of-concept never becomes full deployment.

To unlock the full benefits of predictive maintenance—strategic asset health, global cost reduction, and organization-wide uptime optimization—leaders must **plan for scale from the beginning**. This section explains how to move from isolated pilots to robust, repeatable, enterprise-wide programs.

Why Scale Matters

While a single predictive model on one asset may yield local gains, the exponential value of predictive maintenance emerges when:

- Insights flow across sites, lines, and teams

- Failure patterns in one location inform others

- Procurement and inventory are coordinated based on system-wide intelligence

- Model retraining becomes centralized, standardized, and agile

- The organization speaks a common "health language" for its assets

In essence, **scaling turns data into strategy.**

Step 1: Standardize Infrastructure and Data Models

Scaling requires consistency. If every site uses different sensors, naming conventions, timestamp formats, or CMMS tags, models won't generalize.

Actions:

- Define a common sensor framework and installation guide

- Establish shared naming schemas for assets, parts, and failure modes

- Use consistent time zones, formats, and sampling intervals

- Implement a unified asset hierarchy (line > machine > component)

- Store data in centralized lakes or federated platforms with secure access controls

Example:
A global packaging company harmonized its sensor data streams across 12 plants, enabling

centralized AI models to predict belt failures across all lines with a single system.

Step 2: Build a Scalable Architecture

Tech architecture should be modular, layered, and interoperable—ready to support more assets, more sites, and more users without full redesign.

Key Requirements:

- Scalable cloud infrastructure (multi-site data ingestion and model training)

- Edge devices for local inference and fail-safe alerts

- Integration APIs with CMMS, MES, ERP, and SCADA systems

- Role-based access and permissions for operations, engineering, and analytics

- Data pipelines that are automated, auditable, and fault-tolerant

Tip: Choose platforms with industrial focus and proven success in multi-site deployments.

Step 3: Create a Center of Excellence (CoE)

A dedicated team should oversee the expansion of predictive maintenance—ensuring consistency, quality, and institutional learning.

Core CoE Functions:

- Model validation and retraining across diverse contexts

- Internal consulting for plant-level deployments

- Success metric tracking (uptime, savings, adoption)

- AI governance (ethics, drift detection, risk mitigation)

- Vendor and partner management

Staffing:
Include reliability engineers, data scientists, change managers, and plant champions from multiple geographies.

Quote:

> "Our AI CoE is the bridge between frontline wisdom and data science horsepower."

Step 4: Prioritize Assets and Sites Strategically

Not all machines or locations need predictive maintenance right away. Scaling requires **prioritization based on ROI, risk, and readiness.**

Prioritization Criteria:

- Asset criticality (financial, operational, safety)

- Historical failure patterns

- Availability of data and sensor readiness

- Workforce openness and AI literacy

- Strategic importance (flagship lines or export dependencies)

Example Rollout Plan:

1. Start with flagship site and high-criticality assets

2. Expand to sister lines using transferable models

3. Broaden to diverse geographies, adapting for environmental and cultural variance

4. Use results to guide corporate policy on maintenance funding and uptime targets

Step 5: Create Learning Loops and Feedback Culture

Scaling isn't just about technology—it's about enabling people to continuously improve the system.

What to enable:

- Operators flagging false positives and missed events

- Technicians submitting feedback via mobile apps or digital twins

- Engineers adjusting thresholds and contextual rules based on plant realities

- Maintenance planners reviewing system suggestions during weekly planning

Tip: Reward local teams that contribute to improving central models. They're your intelligence network.

Step 6: Monitor, Measure, and Report at Scale

Without visibility into what's working, what's failing, and what needs tuning, scaling will stall.

KPIs to Track:

- Uptime and Mean Time Between Failure (MTBF) improvements

- Number of alerts generated vs. acted upon

- Number of false positives per asset type

- Cost savings vs. pilot baseline

- User adoption rates across functions

Use dashboards that aggregate local and global metrics while allowing drill-down for root cause investigation.

Step 7: Future-Proof the System

Scaling predictive maintenance should align with your broader digital transformation vision.

Future-Proofing Includes:

- Enabling model interoperability with future AI initiatives (e.g., quality, energy)

- Keeping data ownership clear and compliant (GDPR, ITAR, ISO 27001)

- Designing for multilingual, multicultural global workforces

- Planning for AI model version control and rollback

- Including predictive health scores in executive decision tools

Summary

Scaling predictive maintenance isn't a technical upgrade—it's an organizational transformation. It requires architecture, alignment, and agility.

Start by thinking small. Succeed locally. But always design for global impact.

In the final section of this chapter, we'll tie everything together with a chapter conclusion—revisiting the why, how, and what next of predictive maintenance in your AI manufacturing journey.

Conclusion: Turning Foresight Into Factory Power

Predictive maintenance represents one of the most tangible, transformative applications of AI in modern manufacturing. It takes the age-old challenge of keeping machines running—and reimagines it as a data-driven, foresight-enabled discipline. What was once reactive becomes proactive. What was once guesswork becomes precision.

Throughout this chapter, we've explored the full lifecycle of predictive maintenance:

- **The maturity model** that maps how organizations move from reactive to prescriptive.

- **The technologies**—from sensors and edge computing to AI models and digital twins—that make prediction possible.

- **The modeling process**, from data collection to training, deployment, and continuous improvement.

- **The ROI drivers**, including cost savings, uptime improvements, energy efficiency, and asset longevity.

- **Industry-specific insights**, illustrating how predictive maintenance adapts to different sectors and needs.

- **Challenges and solutions**, covering real-world roadblocks from data gaps to workforce hesitation.

- **The human dimension**, where technicians become strategic reliability partners, not sidelined by automation.

- **Scaling strategies** that turn pilot successes into enterprise-wide transformation.

What emerges is not just a toolkit—but a new philosophy of maintenance. One that's intelligent, adaptive, collaborative, and aligned with the strategic goals of the business.

Beyond Uptime: Strategic Advantages

Predictive maintenance does more than keep machines running. It improves decision-making, accelerates digital maturity, and lays the foundation for broader AI-powered operations.

- It **frees up human potential**—letting your most experienced personnel work on innovation instead of interruption.

- It **fosters cross-functional alignment**, as IT, OT, maintenance, and leadership work toward shared goals.

- It **cultivates a data culture**, where every alert is an opportunity and every insight is a lever.

- And most of all, it **builds resilience**—so that your factory can respond to market changes, supply chain shocks, and rising customer expectations without breaking stride.

Looking Ahead

Predictive maintenance is often the **first successful AI use case in a factory**—but it should never be the last. Once the groundwork is laid, the same principles can be extended to:

- Quality prediction

- Energy optimization

- Production planning

- Inventory intelligence

- Sustainability and compliance

The road to intelligent manufacturing begins with a single model—but it scales to redefine how the entire enterprise thinks, acts, and grows.

3.0 Introduction: Redefining Quality with Intelligence

In manufacturing, **quality is everything**. It determines not only customer satisfaction but also compliance, cost, brand reputation, and operational efficiency. A single defect can ripple through the supply chain—triggering recalls, warranty claims, or customer churn. And yet, despite decades of investment in Six Sigma, lean methods, and automated inspection, quality assurance remains one of the most labor-intensive and error-prone aspects of modern production.

But that is changing.

Artificial intelligence is revolutionizing quality control—not by replacing inspectors, but by enhancing their ability to detect, classify, and prevent defects at scale and speed previously unimaginable. From computer vision systems that identify micro-scratches invisible to the human eye, to predictive models that signal process drift before it affects output, **AI is redefining how manufacturers think about quality—not just as an endpoint, but as an evolving, intelligent process.**

From Detection to Prevention

Traditional quality control methods often fall into two camps:

1. **Manual Inspection:** Visual checks by trained operators. Flexible but inconsistent, subjective, and prone to fatigue-related errors.

2. **Rule-Based Automation:** Pre-programmed inspection systems using hard-coded parameters and thresholds. Consistent but brittle—easily thrown off by lighting, orientation, or product variation.

These systems excel at detection, but they struggle with **adaptation and prediction**. They catch defects after they've occurred, rather than preventing them from emerging in the first place.

AI-based quality control turns this paradigm on its head. By learning from data—thousands of good and bad samples, sensor readings, and process parameters—AI can:

- Detect subtle, previously invisible deviations

- Classify multiple types of defects simultaneously

- Adjust dynamically to new product types or batches

- Trace quality issues back to root causes in real time

- Recommend corrective actions based on historical patterns

The result is a shift from **Quality Assurance to Quality Intelligence**.

Why Now?

While AI for quality has existed in research labs for years, several developments have made it viable—and valuable—on the factory floor today:

- **Camera and Sensor Advances:** Affordable, high-resolution imaging and hyperspectral cameras now capture more detail than ever.

- **Compute Power:** Edge and cloud AI platforms allow real-time model inference and training without high-latency lag.

- **Data Availability:** Most manufacturers now have years of production, inspection, and scrap data—ripe for AI model training.

- **Low-Code Tools:** Engineers and quality managers can now deploy AI solutions without deep programming skills.

- **Standardization and Interoperability:** AI systems can now integrate more easily into MES, PLCs, SCADA, and ERP systems.

Together, these factors make AI a practical tool—not just a futuristic aspiration—for any manufacturer serious about quality.

Chapter Preview

This chapter provides a full-spectrum guide to applying AI in quality control and inspection, including:

- The evolution from visual inspection to AI vision

- The core technologies powering intelligent inspection systems

- How to build, train, and deploy defect detection models

- ROI metrics and business case justification

- Sector-specific case studies: electronics, automotive, packaging, and pharma

- Challenges like false positives, model drift, and operator trust

- The cultural shift from fear of automation to pride in AI-enhanced precision

Whether you're inspecting paint finishes, weld seams, circuit boards, or sterile packaging, this chapter will equip you to lead your organization into the next era of **intelligent, scalable, and proactive quality management.**

3.1 The Evolution of Inspection: From Eyes to AI

The history of quality control is a story of progressive refinement—from subjective judgment to objective measurement, and now to intelligent automation. At each stage, the goal remains the same: to ensure that what is produced meets what was intended. But the methods—and their reliability—have changed drastically.

This section traces the **evolution of inspection in manufacturing**, illustrating the limitations of traditional approaches and why AI represents not just the next step, but a categorical leap forward.

Phase 1: Manual Inspection – Human Eyes, Human Judgment

For centuries, visual inspection by skilled operators was the gold standard in quality control. Whether checking the stitching on fabric, the finish on a machined part, or the alignment of components on an assembly line, humans were the inspectors of record.

Strengths:

- Highly adaptable to new products

- Able to recognize irregularities without formal definitions

- Capable of context-aware judgment

Limitations:

- Subjective and inconsistent across inspectors

- Prone to fatigue, distraction, and lighting conditions

- Difficult to scale across high-volume production

- Challenging to trace or document errors systematically

Example:
In a furniture factory, a final assembly worker examines each chair for wobble, misalignment, or visible defects. Their experience counts—but so do their energy levels, mood, and lighting conditions.

Phase 2: Rule-Based Automation – Consistent, but Rigid

As manufacturing scaled in the 20th century, companies turned to **automated inspection systems** to improve speed and repeatability. These systems used fixed logic: pre-set parameters for color, size, contrast, or edge detection. If a part deviated from the parameters, it was flagged or rejected.

Common Technologies:

- Optical comparators

- Light curtains and photodetectors

- Machine vision with simple thresholding algorithms

- 2D barcode or pattern recognition

Strengths:

- High-speed and consistent

- Good for well-defined, repeatable defects

- Reduces reliance on human labor

Limitations:

- Can't adapt to variations in lighting, background, or part orientation

- Fails with slight misalignments or surface noise

- Struggles with complex or evolving defect types

- High setup time when switching SKUs or product families

Example:
In a beverage plant, a vision system checks fill levels based on a fixed threshold of pixels. Any deviation—due to bottle transparency or camera angle—leads to false positives or missed defects.

Phase 3: Statistical Process Control (SPC) – Looking at the Process, Not Just the Product

In parallel, the rise of **Six Sigma and Total Quality Management (TQM)** brought attention to monitoring the process itself, not just inspecting finished goods. Control charts, process capability indices, and sampling plans became essential tools.

Strengths:

- Helps detect drift or variability early

- Focuses on root cause elimination

- Enables continuous improvement culture

Limitations:

- Relies on aggregate or sampled data

- Can miss rare or batch-specific defects

- Often disconnected from real-time operations

- Requires statistical literacy for interpretation

Example:
In a plastics facility, SPC charts indicate rising variation in mold temperature—hinting at impending warpage issues. However, the charts don't pinpoint which parts are affected or whether the problem is visual.

Phase 4: AI-Powered Inspection – Intelligent, Scalable, Adaptable

AI, especially deep learning, has transformed quality inspection from rule-based logic to **pattern-based understanding**. Convolutional Neural Networks (CNNs) can analyze thousands of defect and non-defect images to learn subtle features, enabling real-time classification and anomaly detection.

Key Capabilities:

- Learn directly from examples (not programmed thresholds)

- Handle complex, multi-type defects across surfaces or forms

- Adapt to noise, lighting, or part rotation

- Continuously improve with more data

AI Techniques in Use:

- Image classification: Is this part defective or not?

- Object detection: Where is the defect located?

- Semantic segmentation: Which pixels belong to a defect region?

- Anomaly detection: What doesn't look like a normal part, even if never seen before?

Example:
An electronics manufacturer trains a deep learning model on 10,000 PCB images. The AI can now spot solder defects, missing components, and incorrect placements—even those it hasn't seen before—at a speed of 40 parts per second.

Comparative Overview

Approach	Adaptability	Speed	Consistency	Setup Effort	Scalability
Manual Inspection	High	Low	Low	Low	Poor
Rule-Based Automation	Low	High	High	High	Limited
Statistical Control	Medium	Medium	High	Medium	Moderate
AI-Based Inspection	Very High	Very High	Very High	Medium	Excellent

Summary

Inspection has come a long way—from a human-centric art to a digitally-empowered science. But AI doesn't just replace human judgment—it scales it, sharpens it, and makes it traceable and repeatable.

This evolution unlocks not just better defect detection—but a **new vision of quality** that is continuous, intelligent, and adaptive.

In the next section, we'll explore the core technologies that make this vision possible—from computer vision and deep learning to multispectral imaging and edge AI.

3.2 Technologies Powering AI-Based Inspection

The success of AI in quality control depends on a sophisticated interplay of hardware and software, data and computation, optics and intelligence. This section breaks down the key technologies that make AI-based inspection possible—each component contributing to faster, smarter, and more reliable defect detection.

From cameras that see beyond the visible spectrum to neural networks that learn from millions of samples, these technologies are **the eyes and brain of intelligent inspection systems**.

1. Computer Vision Systems

Computer vision is the foundation of AI-based inspection. It allows machines to interpret images and video frames, mimicking (and often surpassing) human sight in accuracy and scale.

Core Tasks in Vision-Based Inspection:

- **Classification:** Determining whether an item is good or defective

- **Localization:** Pinpointing where the defect is

- **Segmentation:** Identifying the exact pixels or regions that represent a defect

- **Tracking:** Following objects through a production process for continuity

Tech Stack:

- Industrial-grade cameras (monochrome or color)

- Lens systems optimized for distance, field of view, and distortion correction

- Lighting modules to eliminate glare and shadows

- Image acquisition cards (frame grabbers)

AI Integration:
Captured images are fed into trained neural networks that classify, detect, or segment defects based on learned patterns—not just pre-set rules.

2. Deep Learning and Neural Networks

Unlike traditional vision systems that rely on handcrafted features (e.g., edge detectors, contrast filters), deep learning models **learn features automatically** from labeled data.

Most Common Architectures:

- **Convolutional Neural Networks (CNNs):** For 2D image processing

- **YOLO / SSD / Faster R-CNN:** For object detection and real-time localization

- **U-Net / Mask R-CNN:** For pixel-wise segmentation of complex defects

- **Autoencoders:** For anomaly detection without labeled defects

- **Vision Transformers (ViT):** For high-accuracy classification with less inductive bias

Training Requirements:

- Large, labeled datasets of good and defective parts

- Diverse samples with variation in lighting, angle, and defect type

- GPU-based compute platforms for accelerated model training

Example:
A CNN trained on 15,000 images of tablet coatings detects chipping, discoloration, and contamination with 98.7% accuracy—exceeding human inspection performance under controlled conditions.

3. Multispectral and Hyperspectral Imaging

Standard cameras capture light in the visible spectrum (RGB). But some defects—such as material inconsistencies, chemical residues, or contamination—are invisible to the naked eye.

Multispectral Imaging (MSI): Captures data at a few specific wavelengths (e.g., UV, IR, NIR).
Hyperspectral Imaging (HSI): Captures a full spectral signature at each pixel—often over 100+ bands.

Applications:

- Detecting bruises under the skin of fruits

- Identifying moisture variation in pharmaceuticals

- Verifying plastic type or fiber composition

- Detecting surface contamination or heat damage

AI's Role:
Hyperspectral data is high-dimensional. AI models reduce and analyze this data using dimensionality reduction, clustering, and classification techniques.

4. Edge AI and On-Device Inference

Real-time inspection often requires **decisions in milliseconds**, without round-tripping data to the cloud. That's where edge computing comes in.

Edge AI Devices:

- Compact inference chips (e.g., NVIDIA Jetson, Intel Movidius)

- Smart cameras with onboard compute

- FPGA/ASIC hardware for ultra-low-latency environments

Advantages:

- Instant feedback for defect rejection or line stopping

- Improved data privacy and security

- Lower bandwidth requirements

- Increased system robustness in low-connectivity zones

Example:
A packaging line uses edge-deployed AI to inspect 250 items per minute, identifying seal defects and misprints without needing cloud access.

5. Industrial Connectivity and Integration

No inspection system operates in isolation. AI must be integrated with:

- **Manufacturing Execution Systems (MES):** To log defect rates, tie inspections to batches

- **Programmable Logic Controllers (PLC):** For real-time response (e.g., reject actuator)

- **Supervisory Control and Data Acquisition (SCADA):** For visualizing trends over time

- **Enterprise Resource Planning (ERP):** For linking quality data to customer orders, compliance reports, and recalls

Interoperability Standards:

- OPC-UA

- MQTT

- RESTful APIs

- Digital I/O for real-time signaling

Integration ensures that AI-driven insights turn into action, whether that's rejecting a product, triggering a process adjustment, or initiating a maintenance request.

6. Annotation Tools and Data Management

AI is only as good as the data it's trained on. That's why labeling tools, version control systems, and dataset management platforms are critical.

Annotation Tools:

- Labelbox, CVAT, Supervisely, Roboflow

- Support for bounding boxes, segmentation masks, classification tags

- Batch labeling and QA features

Data Practices:

- Store balanced sets of defect and non-defect images

- Track dataset versions, annotation history, and model lineage

- Capture metadata (e.g., operator ID, line speed, temperature) for correlation

Tip: Treat your training data like your most valuable asset—it is.

Summary

AI-based quality control is built on a sophisticated stack of technologies that combine the best of imaging, intelligence, integration, and inference.

When properly orchestrated, these technologies deliver a system that sees more, learns faster, adapts instantly, and improves continuously.

Next, we'll explore **how to build and train your own AI quality inspection system**—from dataset creation to model deployment and feedback loops.

:

3.3 Building an AI Inspection System: A Step-by-Step Guide

Deploying an AI-driven inspection system is not just a matter of installing cameras and loading software. It involves a series of deliberate, interconnected steps—from selecting the right inspection task to curating datasets, choosing models, and integrating with shop floor operations. Done right, it creates a feedback-driven, continuously improving quality intelligence system.

This section offers a **step-by-step blueprint** for building and operationalizing an AI inspection solution in manufacturing.

Step 1: Define the Use Case

Before collecting data or training models, clearly define what you're trying to inspect, detect, or prevent.

Key Questions:

- What defect(s) are we targeting?

- What's the impact of missing a defect (cost, safety, compliance)?

- Is this a binary classification (good/bad) or multi-defect labeling?

- What is the required inspection speed (parts per minute)?

- What action should the system take upon detection?

Example Use Cases:

- Detect scratches on automotive panels

- Verify correct labeling on pharmaceutical bottles

- Classify welding seam quality as pass/marginal/fail

- Count number of drilled holes on a PCB

Step 2: Capture Representative Data

AI models need lots of examples to learn. Collect a **diverse, labeled dataset** that reflects the full range of real-world conditions.

Best Practices:

- Use consistent lighting and camera positioning

- Capture a mix of defect types and normal parts

- Include edge cases: borderline defects, process drift, machine noise

- Vary conditions: shifts, operators, lighting angles, surface finishes

- Label data using QA-approved annotations

Tip: A dataset with 5,000–10,000 images can yield good results. More is better, especially for rare defects.

Step 3: Annotate the Data

Precise annotations are the foundation of model learning.

Annotation Types:

- **Classification:** Label whole image as defective or not

- **Object Detection:** Draw bounding boxes around defects

- **Semantic Segmentation:** Outline pixel-level defect regions

- **Anomaly Detection:** Provide only good samples; model learns what's "normal"

Tools:

- Labelbox

- CVAT

- Roboflow

- Supervisely

- Custom-built tools with tailored workflows

Quality Checks:

- Use double-pass reviews to catch labeling errors

- Involve domain experts to confirm borderline cases

- Maintain metadata (operator, batch, timestamp) for analysis

Step 4: Train the AI Model

With annotated data ready, it's time to train your model.

Model Choices:

- **CNNs:** Great for image classification

- **YOLO / SSD:** Fast object detection

- **U-Net / DeepLab:** Detailed segmentation tasks

- **Autoencoders:** Ideal for anomaly detection without labeled defects

Training Guidelines:

- Split data into training (70%), validation (20%), and test (10%) sets

- Use data augmentation to simulate real-world noise (rotation, blur, brightness)

- Monitor performance using metrics: accuracy, precision, recall, F1 score, IoU (for segmentation)

Training Tools:

- TensorFlow / Keras

- PyTorch

- OpenCV + scikit-learn

- Google AutoML Vision or Amazon Lookout for Vision (low-code options)

Tip: Always test your model on **real images it has never seen** to validate generalization.

Step 5: Deploy to Production

Once validated, the model must be integrated into the inspection pipeline.

Deployment Approaches:

- **Edge Deployment:** Run model on embedded GPU (e.g., NVIDIA Jetson)

- **Smart Cameras:** Integrate directly into optical hardware

- **On-Premise Server:** Good for plants with strong local infrastructure

- **Cloud Inference:** Useful for batch processing or when latency isn't critical

System Requirements:

- Live video/image feed

- Model inference engine (TensorRT, OpenVINO, or ONNX)

- Threshold configuration (when to trigger alarms)

- Output relay to actuators, alarms, dashboards, or MES

Step 6: Integrate with Plant Systems

AI inspection shouldn't sit in a silo—it must connect to operational systems to drive decisions.

Integration Points:

- **PLCs:** For pass/fail signals, conveyor routing, or reject triggers

- **MES/SCADA:** To log defects per batch, per line, per time window

- **ERP/QA Tools:** For triggering holds, reporting trends, or initiating corrective actions

- **CMMS:** To log inspection-related faults or maintenance alerts

Example Integration:
An AI system detecting label misalignment sends a trigger to a PLC, which diverts the faulty unit. Simultaneously, the MES logs the event and updates a KPI dashboard.

Step 7: Monitor and Improve Continuously

AI systems must be monitored and retrained as conditions change.

Key Metrics:

- True positives (correctly detected defects)

- False positives (false alarms)

- False negatives (missed defects)

- Model confidence levels

- Impact on scrap rate, rework time, or customer returns

Feedback Loops:

- Allow operators to confirm or override AI decisions

- Use flagged images to retrain and improve the model

- Monitor model drift with monthly validation sets

Tip: Build a culture where AI inspection isn't final—it's a learning partner that improves with every shift.

Summary

Building an AI inspection system is a structured, iterative process—anchored in real use cases, grounded in good data, and driven by human-machine collaboration.

It's not just about defect detection—it's about enabling **data-informed production, continuous learning, and scalable quality**.

In the next section, we'll quantify the value this brings—with ROI calculations, KPI tracking, and real examples of measurable improvements in AI-driven inspection.

3.4 ROI and Impact of AI-Driven Quality Systems

Investing in AI for quality control is no longer a speculative bet—it's a measurable, high-yield upgrade with **clear operational and financial returns**. Organizations that deploy AI-driven inspection systems routinely report improvements not only in defect detection but also in scrap reduction, rework costs, labor optimization, and customer satisfaction.

This section examines the **real-world return on investment (ROI)** from AI inspection, exploring where value is created and how to calculate it in meaningful, boardroom-ready terms.

Key Value Areas

1. Improved Defect Detection Accuracy

Traditional inspection methods miss subtle or rare defects due to human fatigue, lighting variability, or camera misalignment. AI improves both **precision (fewer false alarms)** and **recall (fewer missed defects)**.

- **Impact:** Up to 90% reduction in missed critical defects

- **Outcome:** Fewer warranty claims, safer products, improved brand trust

Example:
An auto parts manufacturer reduced undetected weld cracks by 78% after deploying AI-enhanced vision, leading to a 42% decrease in post-shipping returns.

2. Reduction in Scrap and Rework

AI systems detect issues earlier in the production process—often mid-process or even pre-process—reducing the amount of material and labor wasted on defective parts.

- **Impact:** 10–30% reduction in scrap rates

- **Outcome:** Significant cost savings in raw material, labor, and energy

Example:
A precision electronics company saved over $1.2M annually by using AI to identify early-stage soldering defects, cutting rework by 50% and scrap by 22%.

3. Labor Efficiency and Redeployment

AI doesn't eliminate jobs—it reallocates human resources from tedious, repetitive inspection tasks to higher-value roles in root cause analysis, continuous improvement, and process control.

- **Impact:** Up to 60% reduction in manual inspection time

- **Outcome:** Improved workforce engagement and productivity

Example:
A food packaging firm redeployed 12 quality inspectors to preventive maintenance roles after AI systems automated seal and label inspection across three lines.

4. Faster Line Speeds and Throughput

AI-enabled systems can inspect at speeds no human could match—identifying flaws in milliseconds with real-time decision output.

- **Impact:** 5–15% increase in throughput due to reduced bottlenecks

- **Outcome:** Higher daily output, lower per-unit inspection cost

Example:
A glass bottle manufacturer increased line speed by 8% while improving defect detection after replacing slow vision logic with edge-deployed AI.

5. Enhanced Traceability and Compliance

AI systems generate rich data trails—including images, timestamps, defect type, severity, and batch ID—which support audits, recalls, and root cause investigations.

- **Impact:** Full traceability on 100% of production

- **Outcome:** Regulatory compliance, reduced liability exposure

Example:
A pharmaceutical packager passed a critical FDA inspection with zero observations due to AI-generated logs that detailed every defect detected over the prior 90 days.

Calculating ROI: A Sample Framework

Here's a simple annualized ROI model for a mid-size manufacturer deploying AI inspection:

Value Area	Annualized Benefit
Reduced Scrap and Rework	$350,000
Increased Throughput	$180,000
Labor Savings / Redeployment	$140,000
Warranty and Claim Reduction	$90,000
Compliance and Risk Avoidance	$50,000
Total Benefit	**$810,000**

Investment Costs	Amount
Hardware and Cameras	$120,000
Software and Licensing	$80,000

AI Model Development	$60,000
Integration and Training	$40,000
Total Investment	**$300,000**

ROI = (Benefit – Cost) / Cost = ($810K – $300K) / $300K = 170%
Payback Period: ~5 months

Intangible but Strategic Gains

Some benefits are harder to quantify but equally powerful:

- **Faster onboarding for new products and lines**

- **Improved morale among inspectors relieved from monotonous tasks**

- **Fewer customer complaints and better Net Promoter Scores (NPS)**

- **Reputation gains with regulators and high-value clients**

- **AI readiness across other areas (maintenance, logistics, forecasting)**

These factors contribute to long-term competitiveness—even if not captured on a P&L statement.

Sector Snapshots

Sector	Key AI Quality ROI Metric	Typical Payback Period
Automotive	Warranty cost reduction	4–6 months
Electronics	Yield improvement	3–5 months
Pharma	Regulatory compliance & recalls	5–8 months
Packaging	Labeling error reduction	4–6 months
Aerospace	Inspection documentation automation	6–9 months

Summary

The ROI of AI-driven quality systems is no longer theoretical—it's **proven across sectors, geographies, and production scales**. Whether your focus is cost, compliance, customer satisfaction, or capacity, AI delivers measurable improvement while unlocking strategic transformation.

In the next section, we'll look at **industry-specific applications**—showcasing how leading manufacturers are deploying AI inspection in real-world contexts.

3.5 Industry Applications and Case Studies

Artificial intelligence in quality control is not just a concept—it's already deployed in factories across the globe, detecting defects that humans miss, preventing quality escapes, and enabling predictive insights. However, AI does not take a one-size-fits-all approach. Each industry demands tailored inspection systems that reflect its materials, processes, tolerances, and regulatory demands.

This section highlights **sector-specific applications and case studies**, showing how different manufacturers are applying AI to solve distinct inspection challenges.

1. Automotive: Surface Inspection and Weld Verification

Use Case:
A major automotive OEM deployed an AI-based vision system on its final assembly line to inspect door panels for surface defects, including scratches, dents, and waviness. Another deployment focused on verifying weld seam continuity and identifying microcracks in real time.

Technology Stack:

- High-resolution line scan cameras

- Edge-deployed CNNs for surface variation mapping

- Automated defect classification (cosmetic vs. structural)

- Integration with MES for auto-reject and repair routing

Results:

- 93% defect classification accuracy

- $2.3M/year saved in reduced warranty claims

- Faster production line speeds due to lower rework rates

2. Electronics: PCB Defect Detection and Solder Quality

Use Case:
A global consumer electronics manufacturer used AI inspection on SMT (surface mount technology) lines to detect missing components, tombstoning, cold joints, and solder bridging on printed circuit boards.

Technology Stack:

- Microscopic cameras and AOI (Automated Optical Inspection) retrofitted with AI

- Multi-class deep learning models trained on over 100,000 image samples

- Real-time edge inferencing using NVIDIA Jetson modules

- Feedback loop to adjust solder paste volume and reflow profile

Results:

- 28% reduction in false positives compared to rule-based AOI

- 19% increase in first-pass yield

- Rework cost reduction of $1.1M/year across three factories

3. Pharmaceutical: Packaging and Label Integrity

Use Case:
A contract pharmaceutical packager implemented AI inspection to verify pill blister alignment, foil seal integrity, and 2D barcode legibility across multiple product lines.

Technology Stack:

- Infrared and visible-light dual-camera setup

- Deep learning models for segmentation of foil wrinkles and punctures

- OCR (Optical Character Recognition) integrated with AI for label validation

- Edge-server hybrid architecture for compliance traceability

Results:

- 100% regulatory audit compliance with digital inspection logs

- $500K saved annually by reducing over-inspection and repackaging

- 40% improvement in barcode read success rate, even with worn printers

4. Food and Beverage: Packaging Defect Detection

Use Case:
A global beverage company deployed AI inspection across filling lines to detect label misalignment, underfilling, cap misplacement, and foreign particles in transparent bottles.

Technology Stack:

- High-speed cameras operating at 500 frames/sec

- YOLO-based object detection models for label position and cap skew

- ML-based anomaly detection to spot irregular fill levels

- Integration with reject actuator and line-speed controls

Results:

- 96% accuracy in label defect detection

- Over 400,000 mislabeled bottles rejected before leaving the plant in one year

- Improved brand image and reduced retailer complaints by 73%

5. Aerospace: Composite Material Defect Detection

Use Case:
An aerospace component supplier implemented AI visual inspection for carbon-fiber layups and resin-filled composite parts to identify air pockets, fiber misalignment, and voids.

Technology Stack:

- Hyperspectral cameras capturing 120+ wavelengths

- CNN and 3D reconstruction algorithms to detect internal inconsistencies

- Automated traceability linked to lot numbers and resin batches

- Integration with manual verification stations for flagged parts

Results:

- 85% reduction in destructive testing (saving materials and time)

- Elimination of 2 out of 3 previously undetected delaminations

- Over $1.8M saved annually in scrap and rework prevention

6. Packaging and FMCG: Flexible Packaging Quality

Use Case:

A fast-moving consumer goods (FMCG) company used AI to inspect flexible pouches for defects like incorrect printing, sealing issues, miscut notches, and material tears.

Technology Stack:

- Rolling inspection using area scan cameras

- CNNs trained to distinguish printer smears from ink bleed defects

- Smart rejection mechanism coupled with image logging

- Low-code interface for line supervisors to adjust defect severity thresholds

Results:

- Reduced visual defect escape rate by 92%

- 15% lower packaging waste

- 6-week payback period due to rapid reduction in batch rework

7. Textiles and Apparel: Fabric Inspection

Use Case:
An apparel manufacturer applied AI to inspect dyed and woven fabrics for color inconsistency, pattern deviation, thread pull, and holes.

Technology Stack:

- Multispectral line-scan cameras

- CNNs with attention mechanisms for color pattern recognition

- Real-time feedback to loom or dye bath systems

- Cloud model retraining based on seasonal fabric changes

Results:

- 80% faster defect localization

- Improved defect traceability across dye lots

- Scrap fabric reduction of over 25%, saving $380K/year

Summary

From microelectronics to mega-structures, AI inspection is proving its value in **every sector**—each with unique materials, failure modes, and operational priorities. The key to success is **domain-adapted AI systems**, tuned for the specific visual signatures, defects, and workflows of that industry.

The common thread? Each organization moved beyond static, brittle rules to dynamic, learning-driven inspection—reducing waste, boosting quality, and setting a foundation for AI-powered manufacturing excellence.

In the next section, we'll address the **challenges of implementing AI in quality**, and how to overcome them with process, training, and smart governance.

3.6 Challenges and Limitations of AI in Quality Control

While the benefits of AI-based inspection are substantial, deploying these systems in real-world manufacturing environments is not without challenges. From technical barriers like inconsistent data to cultural resistance among frontline staff, every AI initiative must navigate a mix of visible and hidden complexities.

Understanding these obstacles in advance—and building systems to mitigate them—is critical for sustainable success.

1. Data Quality and Labeling Inconsistencies

The Problem:
AI is only as good as the data it learns from. Poor lighting, inconsistent camera positioning, mislabeled samples, and inadequate variation in training images can all lead to model inaccuracy.

Common Symptoms:

- High false positive or false negative rates

- Models that perform well in the lab but poorly on the line

- Model "surprise" when encountering new product variations

Solutions:

- Use data augmentation (e.g., brightness shifts, rotation) to simulate real-world variation

- Periodically update the dataset with new examples from production

- Invest in rigorous, multi-review annotation processes

- Train models incrementally with continual learning frameworks

Tip: Treat your dataset like production equipment—it needs cleaning, maintenance, and calibration.

2. False Positives and Over-Inspection

The Problem:
AI systems, especially those trained on conservative thresholds, may flag too many acceptable items as defective. This leads to **over-sorting, unnecessary rework**, and loss of confidence in the system.

Common Symptoms:

- Operators ignoring AI alerts

- Rework queues with high pass-through rates

- Excess waste from perfectly functional parts

Solutions:

- Adjust classification thresholds based on business cost (i.e., better to miss a cosmetic defect than stop a line)

- Use multi-stage inspection—e.g., quick AI triage followed by human confirmation

- Retrain models using feedback from borderline cases

- Allow operators to flag and override false positives with visual evidence

Tip: Defect tolerance varies by product and customer—so should your model thresholds.

3. Model Drift and Environmental Changes

The Problem:
Over time, shifts in lighting, equipment wear, material changes, or operator behavior can degrade model accuracy. This is known as **data drift** or **concept drift**.

Common Symptoms:

- Gradual decline in performance

- Increased false alarms during seasonal or shift changes

- Unexplained variation between sites

Solutions:

- Monitor model confidence scores and prediction accuracy over time

- Retrain monthly or quarterly using updated production data

- Use transfer learning to adapt existing models to new environments

- Set up A/B testing for new model versions before deployment

Tip: Models must evolve like your factory—build retraining into your schedule.

4. Difficulty Generalizing Across Lines or Products

The Problem:
A model trained on one product or machine may not work well on another—even if they appear similar. Slight differences in shape, color, or defect type can cause performance drops.

Common Symptoms:

- High variance in accuracy across different product families

- Resistance from new sites to reuse existing models

- Increased effort to "copy-paste" inspection systems

Solutions:

- Modularize your architecture—allow per-line customization with shared core logic

- Build product-specific submodels or use meta-classifiers

- Capture defect metadata (e.g., SKU, batch, line) to inform training

- Use federated learning where models improve globally from local variations

Tip: AI can scale—but only if you plan for variability.

5. Operator Skepticism and Human-AI Misalignment

The Problem:
People may distrust or ignore AI recommendations, especially if early versions were inaccurate or if they feel their expertise is being sidelined.

Common Symptoms:

- Bypassing or disabling AI alerts

- Negative feedback loops—operators correcting AI "mistakes" without reporting them

- Slower adoption in experienced teams

Solutions:

- Involve operators from the beginning of the project

- Run AI in "shadow mode" first to validate predictions without risk

- Build intuitive dashboards with visual explanations for each alert

- Recognize operator input as key feedback for model improvement

Tip: Trust is earned. Start with collaboration, not replacement.

6. Integration and IT Constraints

The Problem:
Even a high-performing AI model can be hampered by poor integration with existing shop floor systems, lack of bandwidth, or IT pushback on security and data access.

Common Symptoms:

- Models that work in pilot but stall at scale

- Delays due to firewall restrictions or incompatible protocols

- Inability to log or act on inspection decisions in real time

Solutions:

- Work closely with IT from the outset—define data flows, access controls, and protocols

- Use industry-standard interfaces (OPC-UA, MQTT, REST APIs)

- Build lightweight edge-first systems to minimize network dependence

- Include cybersecurity reviews in your AI deployment roadmap

Tip: Integration isn't an afterthought—it's half the battle.

7. Regulatory, Ethical, and Privacy Concerns

The Problem:
In highly regulated industries (like pharmaceuticals or aerospace), AI decisions must be explainable and auditable. Some organizations also face privacy issues with image capture and cloud processing.

Common Symptoms:

- Regulatory pushback on black-box systems

- GxP or ISO compliance issues

- Legal concerns around image capture of packaging, logos, or personal data

Solutions:

- Use explainable AI tools (e.g., SHAP, Grad-CAM)

- Implement robust audit trails—store images, decisions, and metadata for every prediction

- Keep image data anonymized and encrypted in transmission and storage

- Document all decision logic and model updates for audit readiness

Tip: Compliance isn't optional—bake it into your architecture.

Summary

AI inspection systems are powerful—but fragile if not built with awareness of real-world complexity. The goal is not just to build a great model—but to create a **resilient system** that learns, adapts, and earns trust over time.

In the final section of this chapter, we'll summarize the key takeaways and look ahead to what intelligent quality will mean in the years to come.

Conclusion: Quality Reimagined

Quality has always been at the heart of manufacturing—but today, the very definition of quality is evolving. In an era of mass customization, global supply chains, and zero-defect expectations, traditional inspection methods simply can't keep up. AI offers not just an upgrade, but a complete reimagining of how quality is defined, monitored, and improved.

This chapter has mapped the full journey:

- From **manual inspection** to **vision-driven, machine-augmented systems**

- From static rule-based logic to **adaptive, learning-based models**

- From catching defects after production to **predicting and preventing them in real time**

We've explored the full ecosystem—cameras, sensors, deep learning, edge inference, cloud analytics, and MES integration—showing how they work in harmony to transform inspection from a cost center into a strategic capability.

The Human + AI Partnership

Importantly, AI doesn't replace the human role in quality—it elevates it.

Technicians become trainers. Inspectors become validators. Engineers become intelligence analysts. Decision-making becomes faster, smarter, and more consistent—backed by evidence, not assumption.

This new era of **Quality Intelligence** is not about removing people from the loop. It's about giving people the tools to make better, faster, and more accurate decisions—at scale.

The Broader Impact

AI inspection also contributes to broader goals:

- **Operational Efficiency:** Higher throughput, lower rework

- **Sustainability:** Less scrap, energy use, and wasted material

- **Customer Satisfaction:** Fewer product escapes, stronger brand loyalty

- **Regulatory Compliance:** Transparent audit trails, digital traceability

- **Workforce Empowerment:** New digital skills, higher-value tasks

And because inspection is one of the most visible, measurable applications of AI, it often acts as a **gateway to broader AI adoption** across the factory—from predictive maintenance to process optimization and supply chain forecasting.

Looking Forward

As AI models become more robust, cameras more powerful, and integration easier, quality control will evolve even further:

- Self-learning inspection systems that improve automatically with each shift

- Multimodal models combining vision, sound, and sensor data

- Augmented reality overlays showing live defect probabilities

- Cloud-based benchmarking across global sites for shared learning

- Autonomous defect correction with real-time robotic intervention

This future isn't theoretical—it's unfolding right now.

4.0 Introduction: The Heartbeat of the Smart Factory

In manufacturing, **planning is everything**. It determines what gets produced, when, how, on which machine, and in what sequence. It balances demand with capacity, aligns material availability with machine readiness, and orchestrates labor, inventory, and logistics into a single rhythm. A single mistake—a late order, a missed setup, a machine clash—can ripple into production delays, cost overruns, or dissatisfied customers.

In traditional factories, production planning and scheduling (PPS) is often a fragile equilibrium—**a spreadsheet labyrinth managed by human intuition, rules of thumb, and last-minute adjustments.**

But today, the complexity of modern operations—mass customization, short product life cycles, global supply chains, tight delivery windows—demands more than human guesswork. Manufacturers now require systems that can **see the whole picture, simulate outcomes, and adapt in real time**.

This is where artificial intelligence is rewriting the playbook.

Why AI for Planning?

Artificial intelligence, powered by machine learning, optimization algorithms, and real-time data, offers the ability to:

- Predict bottlenecks before they happen

- Dynamically adjust schedules based on shop floor disruptions

- Simulate thousands of planning scenarios in minutes

- Optimize objectives like lead time, changeover minimization, or on-time delivery

- Rebalance plans automatically in response to changing demand

In effect, AI turns planning from a static, reactive task into a **living, intelligent system**—continuously learning, adapting, and optimizing for the best possible outcome.

Planning vs. Scheduling: A Quick Clarification

Though often used interchangeably, **planning and scheduling** are distinct:

- **Production Planning** is **strategic**—longer-term decisions about what to produce, in what quantity, and with which resources. It considers sales forecasts, inventory targets, and material availability.

- **Scheduling** is **tactical/operational**—assigning tasks to specific machines or operators at specific times. It deals with actual execution, constraints, and shop floor dynamics.

AI can be applied to both levels:

- At the planning level: AI helps forecast demand, optimize production mix, balance line utilization, and prevent overproduction.

- At the scheduling level: AI dynamically sequences jobs, manages priorities, and responds to breakdowns or late material arrivals.

Challenges in Traditional Planning and Scheduling

Manufacturers have long struggled with the limitations of conventional PPS systems, such as:

- **Manual Data Dependency:** Plans are based on outdated or siloed information.

- **Poor Responsiveness:** Most systems can't adapt in real time to disruptions.

- **Conflicting Objectives:** Trade-offs between cost, speed, and flexibility are hard to balance.

- **Over-Simplified Models:** Many planning tools assume perfect flow and ignore real-world constraints.

- **High Cognitive Load:** Planners juggle thousands of variables without decision support.

The result? Planners spend more time firefighting than optimizing—and the business pays the price in delays, overtime, inventory costs, and missed opportunities.

The Rise of AI-Driven Planning Systems

Today's intelligent PPS platforms, built with AI at their core, offer capabilities that were science fiction a decade ago:

- **Demand-Driven Scheduling:** Plans adapt based on live sales or inventory signals.

- **Constraint-Based Optimization:** AI considers capacity, setup times, tool availability, and energy use simultaneously.

- **Predictive Rescheduling:** If a machine is predicted to fail tomorrow, the schedule is preemptively adjusted.

- **Multi-Objective Optimization:** AI balances conflicting KPIs (cost, speed, quality, carbon footprint) using Pareto analysis.

- **Reinforcement Learning:** Algorithms learn which planning decisions yield the best outcomes under uncertainty.

These systems don't just plan—they **learn, adjust, and improve** every day.

What This Chapter Will Cover

In this chapter, we'll explore:

- The evolution from rule-based to AI-enhanced planning

- Core algorithms behind smart scheduling engines

- Key data sources and integrations

- How AI enables adaptive scheduling in real time

- Industry case studies: automotive, electronics, and batch manufacturing

- How to evaluate and implement AI-powered planning tools

- Human-in-the-loop decision making and trust building

Whether you run a job shop, a high-mix low-volume operation, or a global multi-site network, this chapter will give you the tools to transform planning from a bottleneck into a competitive advantage.

Because in the smart factory, planning isn't just a process—it's the **heartbeat of performance**.

4.1 The Evolution of Production Planning Systems

Production planning has always been at the center of manufacturing—but how it's been done has evolved dramatically. From manual wall charts to complex ERP modules, every generation of planning technology has aimed to better balance supply with demand, resources with requirements, and precision with adaptability.

But as factories become smarter, more dynamic, and data-rich, traditional planning systems increasingly fall short. In this section, we trace the **evolution of production planning systems**, setting the stage for why AI is the inevitable next leap.

Stage 1: Manual and Spreadsheet-Based Planning

Era: Pre-1970s to 1980s
Tools: Paper schedules, whiteboards, ledger books, and spreadsheets

In early manufacturing setups, production planning was done manually. Shop floor supervisors would estimate workloads, assign jobs, and adjust schedules based on daily issues. Planning was heavily dependent on human judgment and tribal knowledge.

Challenges:

- No centralized visibility

- Highly reactive and labor-intensive

- Vulnerable to errors, omissions, and knowledge loss

- Little ability to scale or simulate scenarios

Despite its limitations, manual planning fostered flexibility and local autonomy—but at the cost of inefficiency and poor standardization.

Stage 2: MRP – Material Requirements Planning

Era: 1970s–1980s
Core Idea: Ensure materials and components are available when needed.

Material Requirements Planning (MRP) introduced structured logic to manage inventory and procurement. It calculated the materials needed to produce a product and the timing of their availability based on bills of materials (BOMs) and lead times.

Strengths:

- Improved inventory control

- Enabled centralized planning

- Better procurement coordination

Limitations:

- Ignores resource constraints (machines, labor)

- Doesn't handle real-time changes or disruptions well

- Assumes perfect execution and deterministic lead times

MRP was a step forward—but still primarily a **materials-based view of the world**, not a resource-based or time-based one.

Stage 3: MRP II – Manufacturing Resource Planning

Era: 1980s–1990s
Enhancement: Added capacity planning and shop floor control

MRP II extended MRP by incorporating additional resources—machines, tools, labor, and work centers—into planning. It also added modules for finance, HR, and production, making it a precursor to today's ERP systems.

Benefits:

- Holistic manufacturing coordination

- Introduced finite capacity scheduling

- Enabled cross-functional planning

Limitations:

- Complex implementation and configuration

- Still largely deterministic and rule-based

- Inflexible in fast-changing production environments

MRP II aimed for **vertical integration**, but lacked agility and dynamic responsiveness.

Stage 4: ERP – Enterprise Resource Planning

Era: 1990s–2000s
Expansion: Integrated all core business functions—finance, HR, logistics, procurement, production

ERP systems consolidated operations into a single digital backbone. Leading systems (SAP, Oracle, Microsoft Dynamics) offered powerful modules for planning, scheduling, and execution.

Advantages:

- Unified data platform across departments

- Improved data governance and compliance

- Better standardization across global sites

But...

- Production planning remained **batch-based, rule-driven, and often disconnected from the real-time shop floor**

- Scheduling was often an afterthought or handled outside the ERP

- Changes still required human intervention and could take hours or days to propagate

ERP provided **scale and integration**—but not intelligence or adaptability.

Stage 5: APS – Advanced Planning and Scheduling

Era: 2000s–2010s
 Focus: Optimization algorithms to improve scheduling efficiency

APS systems emerged to address ERP's rigidity in scheduling. These systems use linear programming, heuristics, and constraint-based modeling to find "optimal" sequences for production, changeovers, and capacity balancing.

Notable Capabilities:

- Setup time minimization

- Sequence-dependent scheduling

- What-if scenario simulation

- Capacity-constrained finite scheduling

Shortfalls:

- Models often oversimplified real-world variability

- Optimization required intensive configuration and tuning

- Performance degraded in highly volatile environments

- Static rules couldn't learn or adapt over time

APS added **mathematical rigor**, but not **learning capability**.

Stage 6: AI-Driven Planning and Scheduling

Era: 2015–Present
Core Transformation: From optimization to adaptive intelligence

Modern AI planning systems move beyond fixed rules and static parameters. They ingest historical data, learn from patterns, and adapt dynamically to operational shifts. They integrate deeply with IoT, MES, SCADA, and ERP systems to make real-time decisions across machines, products, people, and priorities.

Breakthrough Features:

- Predictive models for demand, delays, and disruptions

- Reinforcement learning for sequence optimization

- Constraint-aware simulation and rescheduling

- Multi-objective planning (cost, time, carbon, quality)

- Human-AI collaboration interfaces with explainability

AI systems do not just **generate better plans**—they do so continuously, at scale, under uncertainty, and with feedback.

Summary

The journey from paper-based planning to AI-powered optimization reflects the growing **complexity of modern manufacturing**—and the growing need for intelligence that is fast, flexible, and data-driven.

AI represents not just a new tool—but a fundamentally different approach: **one that learns, adapts, and improves over time.**

In the next section, we'll explore the **core technologies and algorithms** that power these intelligent planning systems—demystifying the AI inside the engine.

4.2 The Core Algorithms Behind Intelligent Scheduling

Behind every AI-powered production planning system lies a powerful engine of algorithms—mathematical models and learning frameworks that process constraints, optimize trade-offs, and continuously adapt to changing factory realities.

Understanding these algorithms is key to knowing **what's possible**, **how AI makes decisions**, and **where human oversight should be applied**.

This section explores the foundational technologies driving intelligent scheduling—bridging the gap between theory and the shop floor.

1. Constraint-Based Optimization (CBO)

Core Idea:
Plan and schedule tasks while satisfying a set of hard and soft constraints.

Constraints May Include:

- Machine availability

- Setup/changeover time

- Operator skill sets

- Tooling or fixture limitations

- Maximum load or capacity

- Priority orders or delivery deadlines

How It Works:
CBO uses solvers to generate feasible schedules that satisfy all constraints. When multiple feasible solutions exist, it selects the one that best meets objectives (e.g., minimal idle time, minimal lateness, balanced utilization).

Common Techniques:

- Mixed-Integer Linear Programming (MILP)

- Constraint Satisfaction Problems (CSP)

- Disjunctive Graphs for job shop models

Use Case Example:
A steel mill must schedule 40 rolling jobs on 6 mills while minimizing furnace energy usage, respecting coil size constraints, and avoiding back-to-back grade changes.

2. Heuristics and Metaheuristics

Core Idea:
When problems are too complex for exact solutions in reasonable time, use rules of thumb or search-based techniques to find good (not necessarily perfect) answers quickly.

Heuristic Examples:

- Shortest Processing Time (SPT)

- Earliest Due Date (EDD)

- Least Slack Time

Metaheuristic Algorithms:

- Genetic Algorithms (GA): Evolve better schedules by mimicking natural selection.

- Simulated Annealing: Explore the solution space while avoiding local minima.

- Tabu Search: Avoid repeating solutions by maintaining a memory structure.

Use Case Example:

An electronics assembler uses a genetic algorithm to sequence over 200 PCB jobs daily, minimizing setup time while balancing workload across 8 lines.

Strength:

Fast, flexible, scalable to large problem sizes.

Limitation:

May require tuning and lacks guaranteed optimality.

3. Reinforcement Learning (RL)

Core Idea:
Let the AI agent learn optimal scheduling policies by trial and error—rewarding good decisions and penalizing bad ones over thousands of iterations.

How It Works:

- The environment is modeled as a Markov Decision Process (MDP).

- The agent selects actions (e.g., assigning job X to machine Y).

- The environment responds with a new state and a reward (e.g., time saved, throughput improved).

- Over time, the agent learns policies that maximize cumulative reward.

Popular Algorithms:

- Q-Learning

- Deep Q Networks (DQN)

- Proximal Policy Optimization (PPO)

- Actor-Critic Models

Use Case Example:
A packaging plant trains an RL model to dynamically reschedule production during machine failures. The AI learns to minimize downstream disruption by reshuffling non-critical jobs.

Strength:
Adaptive and excellent for complex, high-variability environments.

Limitation:
Training takes time, and decisions may initially appear non-intuitive.

4. Neural Networks and Predictive Modeling

Core Idea:
Use machine learning to predict critical inputs to scheduling—like machine breakdown probability, production time variability, or demand spikes.

Common Applications:

- Forecasting demand to pre-generate production plans

- Predicting order tardiness risk

- Estimating tool wear and scheduling replacements

- Learning from historical scheduling outcomes

Techniques Used:

- Feedforward Neural Networks

- Recurrent Neural Networks (RNNs)

- Long Short-Term Memory (LSTM) models

- Gradient Boosted Trees and Random Forests

Use Case Example:
A contract manufacturer uses LSTM networks to predict production delays based on historical data, weather, operator absenteeism, and supplier delivery times. These insights feed into its dynamic scheduling engine.

5. Multi-Objective Optimization (MOO)

Core Idea:
Most real-world scheduling problems don't have just one objective. AI models must balance competing goals—like cost, time, energy, and quality.

How It Works:

- Uses Pareto Optimization to identify solutions that can't be improved on one objective without worsening another.

- Provides planners with a set of optimal trade-off options (the Pareto front).

Typical Objectives:

- Minimize makespan

- Maximize resource utilization

- Reduce energy consumption

- Improve on-time delivery

- Minimize overtime or labor cost

Use Case Example:
A pharmaceutical firm uses multi-objective AI scheduling to balance GMP-compliant batch sequencing, minimize cleaning time between batches, and align with QA personnel availability.

6. Hybrid AI Systems

Core Idea:
Combine multiple AI and optimization techniques to handle real-world complexity and scale.

Examples:

- A predictive model forecasts late deliveries, which triggers a reinforcement learning-based rescheduler.

- Heuristics are used for daily plans, with CBO engines verifying feasibility overnight.

- Neural networks provide real-time priority scores, feeding a metaheuristic scheduler.

Strength:
Hybrid systems combine speed, intelligence, adaptability, and transparency.

Limitation:
More difficult to maintain and explain—requires skilled AI governance.

Summary

AI scheduling isn't just about faster number crunching—it's about **smart decision-making at scale**. By integrating predictive models, optimization engines, learning agents, and business rules, intelligent planning systems can adapt to real-world uncertainty with elegance and power.

In the next section, we'll explore the **key data inputs and system integrations** that fuel these algorithms—because even the smartest AI needs the right information to perform.

4.3 Data Inputs and System Integration for Smart Planning

The intelligence of any AI-powered scheduling system is only as good as the **data that feeds it**. In modern manufacturing, where complexity reigns and agility is everything, the ability to pull accurate, real-time data from across the enterprise is a defining success factor.

This section breaks down the **core data sources**, their importance, and how smart planning systems integrate with everything from sensors on the shop floor to ERP and CRM platforms in the boardroom.

Why Data Matters

Production planning doesn't happen in a vacuum. It's affected by every variable across the supply chain:

- Machines that break down

- Customers that change orders

- Raw materials that arrive late

- Operators that call in sick

- Tools that wear faster than expected

Traditional systems used static rules to cope with this dynamic reality. AI-based planning systems, in contrast, thrive on **live, contextual, multi-source data**. They use it to predict, adapt, optimize, and recover in real time.

Key Data Inputs for AI Scheduling

1. **Order and Demand Data**

- Customer orders, SKUs, due dates, priority flags

- Forecasted demand from sales or marketing systems

- Backlog data and lead time tolerances

Why it matters:
This is the "demand signal" AI uses to understand what needs to be produced, by when, and in what quantities.

2. Bill of Materials (BOM) and Routing Information

- Hierarchical breakdown of components and subassemblies

- Process steps, machine types, labor requirements

- Routing variations by product version or batch size

Why it matters:
BOMs and routings define how a product flows through the plant, and what constraints are introduced at each step.

3. **Inventory and Material Availability**

- Current stock levels (raw, WIP, finished goods)

- Location and movement of materials in real time

- Open purchase orders and delivery schedules

Why it matters:
AI uses this to avoid planning production that can't start due to missing parts, reducing line idling or partial builds.

4. Machine and Tool Availability

- Real-time equipment status from SCADA/MES systems

- Maintenance schedules and downtime forecasts

- Tooling availability, calibration status, and location

Why it matters:
Knowing what machines are ready, under maintenance, or nearing failure allows AI to adjust workloads before disruptions occur.

5. Labor and Skills Matrix

- Shift rosters and attendance

- Operator qualifications and cross-training levels

- Human-machine assignment rules and labor limits

Why it matters:
AI must account for not just machines—but who's available and trained to run them.

6. Quality and Process Data

- Historical yield rates by product, machine, and operator

- Defect trends and rework probability

- SPC (Statistical Process Control) alerts

Why it matters:
This allows AI to assign sensitive or complex jobs to lines with higher yield, boosting overall quality and efficiency.

7. **Sales, CRM, and Customer Constraints**

- Priority customers and SLAs

- Penalties for delays or early delivery

- Order changes in progress

Why it matters:
Customer-facing systems help AI prioritize what really matters—delivering on time, in full, and in sequence.

8. Environmental and Energy Data

- Shift-level energy pricing (peak/off-peak)

- Emissions thresholds or quotas

- Temperature/humidity that may affect product quality

Why it matters:
Green manufacturing initiatives depend on AI's ability to factor in energy cost and carbon footprint during planning.

System Integration: The Digital Thread

To access this wealth of data, AI scheduling systems must connect to a range of enterprise tools:

System	Integration Role
ERP (SAP, Oracle, etc.)	Orders, inventory, BOM, HR, finance
MES (Manufacturing Execution System)	Work-in-progress, routing, downtime
SCADA / IIoT Platforms	Real-time machine status, sensor inputs
CMMS	Maintenance events, tooling readiness
WMS / Logistics	Material flow, delivery timing, storage constraints
CRM	Customer priorities, SLA triggers, complaints

Forecasting Engines	Demand trends, seasonal variations
Energy Management Systems	Cost optimization, green scheduling

Integration Methods:

- RESTful APIs for cloud-based systems

- OPC-UA, MQTT for shop-floor communication

- Data lakes or warehouses for unified historical analysis

- Event-driven architecture (EDA) for real-time alerts and triggers

Edge vs. Cloud: Where the AI Lives

- **Edge Scheduling Engines:**
  Run on local servers or machines—ideal for ultra-low-latency decision-making (e.g., reassigning jobs after a machine fault).

- **Cloud-Based Optimization:**
  Better for large-scale, multi-factory planning that requires global visibility and heavy computation (e.g., master production scheduling across regions).

Hybrid Approaches are increasingly common—combining fast edge response with cloud-scale learning.

Data Governance and Security

AI systems that touch multiple enterprise platforms must be **secure, compliant, and auditable**.

- Role-based access controls

- End-to-end encryption (especially for cloud transmission)

- Audit trails for all decisions and changes

- GDPR and ISO compliance for international sites

Tip: Ensure that every data stream has a defined owner, structure, and update cadence.

Summary

Data is the fuel of intelligent scheduling—and integration is the engine. A smart planning system must **see across the enterprise**, synthesize thousands of signals, and act with full context.

When well-connected, AI becomes not just a planner—but a **strategic conductor**, orchestrating machines, people, materials, and demand into one cohesive flow.

In the next section, we'll see how these systems work in the real world—reacting to changes, recalculating plans, and optimizing outcomes in **real time**.

4.4 Real-Time Scheduling and Adaptive Response

In today's high-mix, fast-paced manufacturing environments, **planning doesn't end once a schedule is published**. Machines fail. Orders change. Operators call in sick. Materials don't arrive on time. These disruptions can throw even the best-laid plans into chaos—unless the system can respond, adapt, and recover instantly.

This is where AI-powered real-time scheduling becomes essential. Unlike static planning tools that require manual rescheduling or nightly batch updates, real-time AI scheduling systems operate as **living systems**—constantly sensing, predicting, and recalculating to ensure operations stay optimized under pressure.

What Is Real-Time Scheduling?

Real-time scheduling refers to the system's ability to:

- Detect disruptions the moment they occur

- Evaluate the impact across orders, resources, and KPIs

- Instantly propose or enact rescheduling options

- Learn from outcomes and improve future responses

It's not just speed—it's **intelligent, context-aware reaction**.

Common Real-Time Triggers

Smart scheduling engines monitor multiple data streams and respond when key changes occur:

Trigger Type	Example Event
Machine Failure	CNC spindle unexpectedly goes offline
Late Material Arrival	Critical part shipment delayed by 8 hours
New Rush Order	Priority job added mid-shift
Operator Absence	Skilled welder unavailable for the day
Yield Drop	Defect rate spikes on a coating line
Tool Unavailability	Fixture required for setup is already in use
Environmental Change	Humidity too high for powder application line

How Real-Time AI Scheduling Works

1. **Continuous Monitoring**

   - Integrates with MES, SCADA, IoT devices, and CMMS

   - Ingests signals: machine status, order queue, WIP levels, operator logs

2. **Event Detection**

   - Detects abnormalities (e.g., deviation from predicted cycle time)

   - Flags downstream effects using dependency graphs or digital twins

3. **Impact Assessment**

   - Calculates how the disruption affects deadlines, setups, utilization

   - Identifies affected orders, machines, shifts, and KPIs

4. Dynamic Re-Scheduling

- ○ Generates multiple alternatives using constraint-based optimization

- ○ Weighs options (e.g., shift jobs, split batches, delay non-urgent work)

- ○ Selects best scenario based on business rules or AI policy

5. Execution and Feedback

- ○ Pushes new instructions to MES or operator dashboards

- ○ Logs decisions for traceability and continuous learning

Real-Time Scheduling in Action: Example Scenarios

Scenario 1: Last-Minute Order Addition

- A customer calls at 10 a.m. requesting 1,000 parts by end-of-day.

- The AI system checks available lines, idle tools, and priority of current jobs.

- It inserts the urgent job between two low-priority runs on Line 4, extending overtime by 20 minutes but meeting all other deadlines.

- Operators are notified instantly on their tablets with updated sequence plans.

Scenario 2: Machine Breakdown

- A critical injection molding machine halts due to a temperature fault.

- The AI model had predicted rising cycle time deviation and already marked the asset as "at risk."

- Upon confirmation of downtime, the scheduler shifts pending jobs to two smaller presses with parallel molds, adjusting batch sizes and setup plans.

- Maintenance is auto-notified, and upstream suppliers are paused to avoid WIP pileup.

Scenario 3: Workforce Shortage

- Two skilled painters are absent for the afternoon shift.

- The system filters available workers and identifies substitutes with partial qualifications.

- It reschedules high-spec coatings to the evening shift and prioritizes low-risk jobs for now.

- Shift supervisor receives updated allocation and justification.

Key Technologies Enabling Real-Time Response

- **Digital Twins** to simulate impact across processes

- **Event-Driven Architecture (EDA)** to trigger recalculation instantly

- **Graph-Based Scheduling Models** that represent dependencies and sequence flexibility

- **Reinforcement Learning Agents** that learn optimal responses from past disruptions

- **Edge AI Inference** to respond within milliseconds without cloud delay

Benefits of Adaptive Scheduling

- **Reduced Downtime:** Immediate rerouting prevents idle machines and labor

- **Higher On-Time Delivery:** Maintains promise dates even during chaos

- **Lower Planner Stress:** Replaces manual adjustments with intelligent suggestions

- **Better Resource Utilization:** Dynamic rebalancing avoids under/overload

- **Increased Agility:** Enables just-in-time responsiveness to market changes

Human-in-the-Loop Collaboration

Real-time scheduling doesn't remove humans—it empowers them. AI proposes and explains changes, but final authority often stays with planners and supervisors.

Features to support this:

- Visual scenario comparison (cost, delay, energy use)

- "What-if" sandboxing for experimentation

- Override options with audit trail

- Transparent confidence scores for each suggestion

This builds **trust in the system**—a critical ingredient in successful AI adoption.

Summary

The factory floor is dynamic. So should be your planning.

AI-driven real-time scheduling enables factories to operate with **resilience, responsiveness, and foresight**. It ensures that plans aren't static blueprints—they're **living maps**, always adapting to keep production flowing smoothly.

In the next section, we'll look at real-world case studies of how manufacturers are deploying adaptive AI planning at scale—turning theory into throughput.

4.5 Case Studies in AI-Driven Production Planning

The true power of AI in production planning is best illustrated through real-world deployments. Across industries, manufacturers are discovering that intelligent scheduling systems offer not just marginal gains—but fundamental improvements in flexibility, speed, and decision quality.

This section explores diverse case studies of **AI-powered planning in action**, showing how factories of every size and complexity are optimizing performance with predictive, adaptive tools.

1. Automotive Supplier: Dynamic Job Shop Scheduling

Context:
A Tier 1 automotive parts supplier was facing daily schedule volatility due to frequent order changes, equipment constraints, and limited operator availability. Traditional ERP and APS tools required hours of manual tweaking per shift.

AI Solution:
A real-time AI scheduling engine was implemented using reinforcement learning to continuously optimize job sequencing across 30+ machines.

Key Features:

- Integrated MES, CMMS, and operator skill matrix

- Re-trained models weekly based on execution feedback

- Included setup time penalties and preventive maintenance windows

Outcomes:

- 22% reduction in average changeover time

- 16% increase in on-time delivery

- 4.8 hours/week reduction in planner intervention

- Payback achieved in under 4 months

2. Electronics Manufacturer: Forecast-Driven Scheduling

Context:
A high-volume PCB assembler struggled with aligning production to volatile customer demand. Sales forecasts were often off by 10–20%, leading to overproduction and backorders.

AI Solution:
An AI-powered planning tool was deployed that linked demand forecasting models to production scheduling. The system used historical data, seasonal patterns, and order velocity to adjust schedules daily.

Key Features:

- LSTM neural network for demand forecasting

- Integrated with SAP ERP and factory MES

- Automatically adjusted job splits across SMT lines

Outcomes:

- Forecast accuracy improved from 80% to 93%

- Inventory carrying costs reduced by $420K/year

- Increased line utilization by 13%

- 98% forecast-based scheduling coverage

3. Pharmaceutical Company: Batch Manufacturing Optimization

Context:
A mid-sized pharmaceutical producer needed to schedule liquid medicine batches across shared equipment while minimizing cleaning time and complying with GMP constraints.

AI Solution:
A constraint-based scheduling engine was developed using a genetic algorithm to optimize sequence based on changeover time, shelf life, and QA availability.

Key Features:

- Modeled product incompatibility rules

- Built-in audit log for validation

- Scenario planner for customer order changes

Outcomes:

- 37% reduction in cleaning cycles

- Batch cycle time dropped by 11%

- Regulatory approval facilitated through explainable AI

- Saved ~$600K/year in wasted API and cleaning solvent

4. Steel Manufacturer: Multi-Objective Optimization

Context:
A large steel producer operated a rolling mill with highly variable job priorities, energy costs, and delivery timelines. Planning required balancing setup time, grade transitions, and electricity pricing.

AI Solution:
A multi-objective optimization engine was implemented using Pareto front analysis to generate scheduling options based on customer priority, energy usage, and equipment efficiency.

Key Features:

- Integration with SCADA and utility energy pricing feeds

- Machine learning model to predict coil surface quality by sequence

- Scenario generation and human-in-the-loop selection

Outcomes:

- 18% energy savings during peak hours

- 9% increase in first-pass yield

- Reduced overtime hours by 21%

- Provided planners with 3–5 Pareto-optimal options daily

5. Furniture Manufacturer: Hybrid Cloud Scheduling

Context:
A make-to-order furniture company had a high SKU mix, low automation, and unpredictable material deliveries. Their Excel-based planning process was unreliable and slow.

AI Solution:
A cloud-based AI planning system was deployed to dynamically sequence jobs across carpentry, upholstery, and finishing areas. Edge devices at each station displayed updated task lists and worker assignments.

Key Features:

- Edge + cloud hybrid architecture

- Daily retraining based on WIP and absenteeism

- SMS alerts to team leads for critical job shifts

Outcomes:

- Lead time cut from 12 to 8 days

- Late deliveries dropped from 19% to 5%

- Enabled 3x faster onboarding of new planners

- 12-month TCO (total cost of ownership) ROI achieved in 6.5 months

6. Consumer Packaged Goods (CPG): Campaign Planning Automation

Context:
A multinational CPG company producing beverages and cosmetics struggled with campaign scheduling—coordinating production runs based on flavor, bottle type, and region while minimizing changeovers.

AI Solution:
An AI-assisted campaign planning engine was built using historical sales, shelf-life constraints, and promotional calendar inputs to create optimal weekly plans.

Key Features:

- Demand segmentation model for product families

- Forecast integration with trade promotion schedules

- Automatic grouping of SKUs to minimize switchovers

Outcomes:

- Changeovers reduced by 34%

- Material wastage down by 12%

- 15% improvement in forecast accuracy for regional campaigns

- Planning cycle time reduced from 6 hours to under 1 hour

Summary

These case studies illustrate that **AI-driven production planning is not a future ambition—it's a present reality**. Whether in discrete manufacturing, batch production, or hybrid operations, organizations that adopt intelligent planning are seeing:

- Faster planning cycles

- Higher schedule reliability

- Leaner operations

- Greater agility and resilience under disruption

Each deployment was tailored to the industry's unique constraints—but shared the same goal: **turning complexity into clarity, and variability into value**.

In the final section of this chapter, we'll distill the key takeaways and provide a roadmap for launching your own AI-powered planning initiative.

Conclusion: From Plan to Precision

In the traditional manufacturing world, planning was often reactive—a paper schedule pinned to a board, a phone call to reschedule an order, a supervisor juggling machines during a late shift. These methods worked when variability was low, products were fewer, and the pace of change was slower.

But in today's factories, where **orders change daily, SKUs multiply monthly, and global disruptions are the norm**, the old playbook no longer applies. Planning must evolve from a static process into a dynamic, intelligent function. This is where artificial intelligence becomes indispensable.

Throughout this chapter, we explored how AI transforms production planning from:

- **Guesswork to intelligence**

- **Schedules to simulations**

- **Reaction to anticipation**

- **Constraint to optimization**

- **Firefighting to foresight**

What We've Covered

- The **evolution** from manual planning and MRP to real-time, AI-augmented systems

- The **core algorithms**—from constraint optimization to reinforcement learning—that power intelligent scheduling

- The **critical role of data** from ERP, MES, sensors, and human inputs

- How real-time systems adapt to disruptions—turning complexity into continuity

- **Case studies** across automotive, pharma, electronics, and CPG industries proving the tangible value of smart planning

The result? Planning becomes a **strategic capability**—fueling throughput, reducing cost, and strengthening customer trust.

A Roadmap for Adoption

For manufacturers ready to begin or accelerate their AI journey in production planning, here's a 6-step adoption framework:

1. Define the Business Goal First

Start not with technology—but with the pain point. Are you trying to reduce changeovers? Improve on-time delivery? Handle more complexity with fewer planners?

2. Audit Your Data Landscape

Map your planning-related data: orders, routings, operator availability, real-time machine status, and inventory. Identify gaps, inconsistencies, or silos.

3. Start with a Pilot

Choose one line, one product family, or one shift. Deploy AI in shadow mode first—running parallel to human planners to validate performance and build trust.

4. Involve the Frontline Early

Planning affects everyone—from supervisors to operators. Involve them in the testing and feedback process. AI should empower their expertise, not bypass it.

5. Build Iteratively

Begin with scheduling automation. Then layer on forecasting, constraint modeling, real-time response, and eventually reinforcement learning. Each level builds on the last.

6. Monitor, Measure, and Improve

Track KPIs like changeover time, order lead time, planner hours, and schedule adherence. Use this feedback to retrain models and refine constraints.

Looking Ahead

AI in planning is not the end goal—it's the beginning of a larger transformation:

- Integration with **supply chain AI** for end-to-end orchestration

- Merging with **quality and maintenance intelligence** to optimize for total equipment effectiveness (OEE)

- Feeding into **energy-aware scheduling** to reduce emissions and manage grid demand

- Empowering **autonomous operations**, where machines and systems self-schedule based on objectives and context

As factories become more connected, modular, and intelligent, planning will no longer be a back-office task—it will be the **orchestrator of agility and advantage.**

5.0 Introduction: Intelligence Across the Chain

The supply chain is no longer just a backend function—it's the lifeline of modern manufacturing. It determines **what you can make, when you can make it, and how competitively you can deliver**. And yet, despite its strategic role, most supply chains still operate in the shadows of spreadsheets, static ERP rules, and yesterday's forecasts.

In today's volatile world—where global disruptions, demand shocks, and geopolitical tremors are the norm—this approach is no longer sustainable.

Enter **artificial intelligence**.

AI is transforming supply chains from brittle and reactive systems into **intelligent, connected ecosystems** that sense disruptions early, predict outcomes accurately, and respond dynamically. From **procurement to last-mile delivery**, AI is powering a new era of end-to-end synchronization and self-correction.

Supply Chains Under Pressure

Even before the COVID-19 pandemic, supply chains were facing a growing set of challenges:

- **Globalization** stretched sourcing across continents, increasing complexity and risk

- **Customization and SKU proliferation** made demand forecasting harder

- **Just-in-time models** left little room for error

- **Trade wars and tariffs** reshaped procurement priorities

- **Sustainability pressures** demanded more transparency and accountability

And then came the pandemic—forcing every manufacturer to rethink resilience, responsiveness, and visibility.

Traditional systems couldn't cope. But AI could.

From Linear Chains to Intelligent Networks

The conventional supply chain is often linear:

Supplier → Manufacturer → Distributor → Retailer → Customer

But AI enables a shift to a **networked model**—where data flows freely, partners collaborate digitally, and decisions are made based on **real-time intelligence**, not delayed reports.

AI transforms the chain into a system that:

- **Predicts disruptions** before they hit

- **Optimizes procurement** in real time based on cost, risk, and carbon

- **Balances inventory** across sites and warehouses

- **Orchestrates logistics** based on capacity, delivery time, and weather

- **Responds autonomously** when things go off plan

It's no longer about managing supply—it's about mastering flow.

What AI Brings to the Supply Chain

Function	Traditional Approach	AI-Powered Approach
Forecasting	Time-series extrapolation	Neural networks + external signal fusion
Procurement	Static contract and price-based	Dynamic supplier scoring and automated negotiation
Inventory	Reorder point logic	Predictive modeling and adaptive buffer control
Logistics	Fixed route and schedule	AI-optimized routing, capacity-aware scheduling
Risk Management	Manual risk registers	Real-time risk sensing and simulation

Chapter Preview

In this chapter, we'll explore how AI is used to revolutionize each key area of the supply chain:

- **Forecasting and demand sensing** using machine learning

- **Supplier selection and performance management** with AI scoring

- **Smart procurement and contract optimization**

- **Inventory right-sizing and stockout prevention**

- **Logistics coordination and route optimization**

- **Risk anticipation and resilience building**

- **End-to-end visibility across the supply chain digital twin**

We'll also include real-world case studies, integration strategies, and a roadmap for launching intelligent supply chain initiatives—whether you're sourcing raw materials, managing warehouses, or delivering to end consumers.

Why It Matters Now

AI in supply chain isn't a future vision—it's a **current necessity**. The manufacturers who survive and thrive in the next decade will be those who can:

- See across their networks

- Predict disruptions

- Optimize decisions

- Respond in real time

- And learn continuously

In the age of uncertainty, intelligence is the ultimate advantage.

5.1 AI in Forecasting and Demand Sensing

At the heart of every efficient supply chain lies a simple but difficult question: **"How much will we need?"** For decades, manufacturers relied on historical sales, rolling averages, and seasonal adjustments to forecast demand. But in today's hyper-dynamic world—shaped by social trends, economic swings, geopolitical events, and climate patterns—these traditional models fall short.

AI changes everything.

By combining machine learning, neural networks, and external signal fusion, **AI forecasting systems learn from the past while adapting to the present**, enabling manufacturers to respond faster and plan smarter.

The Forecasting Challenge

Forecasting is traditionally plagued by three core problems:

1. **Volatility:** Consumer preferences, global events, and market conditions shift rapidly.

2. **Latency:** By the time demand data is collected and processed, it may already be outdated.

3. **Granularity:** Forecasts often fail at SKU, store, or channel levels where actual decisions are made.

Even a 5–10% error in forecasts can lead to:

- **Stockouts**, causing lost revenue and customer dissatisfaction

- **Overstock**, leading to excess carrying costs, obsolescence, and markdowns

- **Inefficient production**, triggered by batch sizes misaligned with real demand

AI mitigates these risks by learning **complex, nonlinear relationships** and adapting continuously.

How AI Forecasting Works

AI-based forecasting combines **historical demand data** with a **wide range of internal and external variables** to generate highly accurate predictions.

Data Sources May Include:

- Point-of-sale (POS) data

- ERP order history

- Marketing promotions and campaign calendars

- Social media sentiment and trends

- Macroeconomic indicators

- Weather forecasts

- Competitor behavior or market signals

AI Models Used:

- **Time Series Models** with deep learning (e.g., DeepAR, Temporal Fusion Transformers)

454

- **Multivariate Regression** and XGBoost for cross-variable relationships

- **Reinforcement Learning** to optimize forecast-driven decisions

- **Ensemble Learning** to combine predictions from multiple models

Forecast Outputs:

- SKU-level, region-level, or customer-specific demand predictions

- Confidence intervals and anomaly detection

- Automatic alerts for forecast deviation

Demand Sensing vs. Demand Forecasting

Forecasting projects future demand based on historical data and known events.
 Demand sensing adjusts that forecast in near real-time using current data signals.

For example:

- A sudden spike in website traffic for a product

- News coverage of a product category

- An unexpected cold front driving sweater sales in October

AI demand sensing engines update forecasts **hourly or daily**, improving short-term accuracy.

Benefits:

- 20–40% more accurate short-term forecasts

- Faster response to demand shifts

- Less reliance on safety stock buffers

Benefits of AI Forecasting

Metric	Traditional Forecasting	AI-Powered Forecasting
Accuracy	70–80%	85–95%
Granularity	Weekly/monthly, product-level	Daily/hourly, SKU-location-level
Responsiveness	Slow to adapt	Near real-time updates
Scenario Planning	Manual only	Automated simulations
Promotions & Cannibalization	Hard to model	Learnable via historical data

Case Example: CPG Demand Surge

A global consumer goods manufacturer deployed AI forecasting across 8 regional business units. During a product relaunch, the model detected unusual search traffic, influencer engagement, and POS spikes—well before traditional systems flagged a trend.

Result:
The company adjusted production allocation within 48 hours, avoiding a projected $2.2M in stockouts across key markets.

Case Example: Industrial Equipment

A manufacturer of heavy construction tools used AI to forecast dealer inventory needs based on:

- Weather patterns

- Regional construction permits

- Infrastructure funding data

This allowed it to shift from push to pull-based production—cutting finished goods inventory by 23% and improving order fulfillment by 19%.

Best Practices for AI Forecasting Deployment

1. **Start with Clean Data**
   Historical order and shipment data should be validated, cleansed, and normalized.

2. **Begin with a Pilot Scope**
   Test on a focused region or product category to validate lift before scaling.

3. **Fuse External Signals**
   Integrate weather, social sentiment, competitor pricing, or events that affect demand.

4. **Use Forecasts as Input, Not Gospel**
   Forecasts should feed into planning—but not override human judgment, especially during anomalies.

5. **Retrain Models Frequently**
   Weekly or even daily retraining ensures relevance in volatile markets.

6. **Create Cross-Functional Visibility**
   Share forecast outputs with sales, marketing, finance, and operations to improve alignment.

Summary

AI forecasting and demand sensing bring manufacturers closer to **what customers actually want—before they even ask**. By fusing data from every corner of the business and the market, these systems generate **more accurate, granular, and dynamic forecasts** than traditional methods ever could.

In the next section, we'll move downstream to explore how AI transforms **procurement and supplier relationship management**—ensuring that what's forecasted can actually be fulfilled, reliably and competitively.

5.2 AI in Procurement and Supplier Optimization

Procurement has long been seen as a cost center—focused on savings, contracts, and compliance. But in a world of supply shocks, raw material scarcity, and mounting ESG scrutiny, procurement is now a **strategic pillar of supply chain resilience**. And artificial intelligence is redefining what's possible.

From real-time supplier scoring to predictive sourcing and autonomous negotiation, AI is transforming procurement into a data-driven, risk-aware, and future-ready function.

The Procurement Bottleneck

Traditional procurement struggles with:

- **Manual processes** (RFQs, bid comparisons, supplier scoring)

- **Lack of visibility** into supplier performance or financial health

- **Static contracts** unresponsive to price or availability changes

- **Slow decision-making** that misses early signals of risk

- **Inability to scale** vendor analysis across thousands of SKUs

AI addresses these issues by introducing speed, intelligence, and strategic foresight—while improving collaboration with vendors and internal stakeholders.

AI Applications in Procurement

Here's how AI enhances every phase of procurement:

---

1. Supplier Discovery and Prequalification

- Uses AI-powered search engines to identify global suppliers based on certifications, capacity, delivery history, and sustainability scores

- Automates vendor onboarding using document classification and entity recognition

Result: Broader, faster discovery with smarter filtering—expanding options without increasing risk.

2. Supplier Scoring and Performance Monitoring

- Tracks on-time delivery, defect rates, response times, and price volatility

- Monitors news, ESG violations, litigation, or credit risks using NLP (Natural Language Processing)

- Scores suppliers dynamically using machine learning models

Example:
A defense manufacturer receives automatic risk alerts when a critical supplier's region faces political unrest—prompting preemptive stockpiling.

3. Predictive Sourcing

- Forecasts material requirements based on AI-driven demand sensing

- Aligns supplier availability with production schedules

- Suggests early procurement for long-lead or at-risk components

Impact: Reduces rush orders, emergency buys, and production delays.

4. Dynamic Contracting and Price Optimization

- Monitors commodity price trends (e.g., steel, semiconductors) in real time

- Uses game theory and AI simulations to model negotiation outcomes

- Recommends contract timing and volume thresholds based on predicted price shifts

Example:
A beverage manufacturer locks in a futures-based packaging contract after AI models project a 14% rise in aluminum costs over the next quarter.

5. Autonomous RFQs and Negotiation

- AI bots issue RFQs, compare quotes, and simulate supplier offers

- Uses reinforcement learning to improve bidding strategy

- Automates low-risk negotiations (e.g., MRO parts, indirect spend)

Result: Procurement teams focus on strategic negotiations, while routine sourcing is handled 24/7 by intelligent agents.

6. Supplier Collaboration and ESG Tracking

- Predicts supplier capacity constraints and proposes co-investment options

- Analyzes emissions data, labor practices, and ethical sourcing compliance

- Generates supplier ESG scorecards for board reporting

Use Case:
A consumer brand uses AI to audit Tier 2 supplier sustainability using satellite data and public reports, improving its Scope 3 emissions accuracy.

Benefits of AI in Procurement

Benefit	Impact
Faster Sourcing	Cut RFQ cycle time by 30–70%
Risk Reduction	Early detection of disruption or compliance issues
Cost Optimization	Dynamic pricing strategies and contract timing
Supplier Diversification	Greater visibility into global options
Data-Driven Strategy	Actionable dashboards and predictive insights
Compliance and ESG Visibility	Automatic audits and performance tracking

Case Study: Global Electronics OEM

Challenge:
The company faced repeated delays due to reliance on three key suppliers in Southeast Asia. Market volatility, power outages, and political unrest worsened delivery timelines.

AI Solution:

- AI scored all Tier 1 and Tier 2 suppliers on delivery risk, exposure, and geographic clustering

- Proposed alternative suppliers from Mexico and Eastern Europe

- Suggested new contract clauses to hedge against weather-related disruptions

Results:

- Lead time volatility cut by 41%

- Supplier diversification increased from 1.8 to 3.2 per component

- Material availability improved by 17%, reducing line stoppages

Case Study: Pharma Procurement Automation

Challenge:
Manual RFQs for packaging materials created bottlenecks in a global pharma company, slowing production of time-sensitive medications.

AI Solution:

- A procurement bot handled RFQ issuance, quote comparison, and initial supplier outreach

- Used NLP to extract key clauses from contracts

- Prioritized suppliers with fastest delivery and best quality scores

Results:

- RFQ cycle time dropped from 7 days to under 2

- On-time delivery rate improved by 22%

- Sourcing team productivity increased by 40%

Implementation Tips

1. **Start Small but Strategic**
   Choose one category—like indirect materials, packaging, or electronics—for your pilot.

2. **Integrate with ERP and Supplier Portals**
   Automate data flow for pricing, lead times, and contracts.

3. **Focus on Data Hygiene**
   Clean supplier master data, unify formats, and tag key risk variables.

4. **Build Trust with Teams and Vendors**
   Ensure AI recommendations are explainable and overrideable. Vendors should view AI as a partner, not a penalty system.

5. **Measure Impact Rigorously**
   Track time-to-source, vendor quality trends, and realized savings vs. predicted.

Summary

AI turns procurement into a **proactive, predictive, and strategic powerhouse**. By automating the routine, augmenting the complex, and anticipating the risky, it gives procurement teams the insights—and the time—they need to focus on what matters most: continuity, cost, and collaboration.

In the next section, we'll explore how AI optimizes **inventory management**—ensuring that what's sourced is always available, but never in excess.

5.3 AI in Inventory Optimization and Stock Management

Inventory is both an asset and a liability. Hold too little, and you risk stockouts, missed sales, and disrupted production. Hold too much, and you tie up working capital, waste warehouse space, and risk obsolescence. Striking the perfect balance has always been the holy grail of supply chain management.

Artificial intelligence is bringing that goal within reach—by enabling **adaptive, data-driven inventory systems** that learn, sense, and self-correct across the supply chain.

Traditional Inventory Models Fall Short

Conventional inventory management relies heavily on fixed rules:

- Min-max levels

- Safety stock buffers

- Reorder points

- EOQ (Economic Order Quantity) formulas

These models assume stable demand, predictable lead times, and static service levels—assumptions that rarely hold true in today's volatile markets. They also struggle to scale across thousands of SKUs, locations, and supply scenarios.

How AI Optimizes Inventory

AI-driven inventory optimization engines use machine learning to understand:

- **How much to stock**

- **Where to position it**

- **When to replenish**

- **How to respond to variability in demand and supply**

Unlike static rules, AI systems:

- Continuously learn from real-world consumption patterns

- Predict future demand with more granularity

- Simulate multiple inventory strategies under uncertainty

- Optimize for objectives like cost, service level, or cash flow

Key AI Techniques Used

1. **Time Series Forecasting:**
   Uses historical consumption data at SKU-location level, adjusting dynamically to trends, seasonality, and promotions.

2. **Monte Carlo Simulation:**
   Models hundreds of scenarios based on uncertainty in demand, lead time, and transit risk.

3. **Reinforcement Learning:**
   Learns the best inventory policy over time by maximizing long-term service level and minimizing holding costs.

4. **Multi-Echelon Inventory Optimization (MEIO):**
   Optimizes stock across the entire supply network—not just one node at a time—accounting for interdependencies.

5. **Anomaly Detection:**
   Identifies demand spikes, order anomalies, or supplier delays before they distort replenishment logic.

Smart Inventory Inputs

To function properly, AI systems ingest data from across the enterprise:

- **Sales and demand forecasts** (SKU-week-store)

- **Order and shipment history**

- **Inventory on hand and in transit**

- **Supplier lead times and performance

- **Product lifecycle stage and seasonality

- **Warehouse and logistics capacity

- **Pricing, promotions, and events**

The broader the context, the smarter the system.

Benefits of AI Inventory Optimization

Metric	Traditional Approach	AI-Driven Approach
Forecast Accuracy	70–80%	85–95%
Service Level	90–93%	96–99%
Inventory Turns	4–6	8–12
Working Capital Tied Up	High	Optimized and targeted
Response Time	Weeks	Real-time or daily updates

Case Study: Retail Chain Optimization

Challenge:
A national apparel chain managed over 20,000 SKUs across 300 stores and 4 DCs. Static rules led to excess stock in low-turn locations and chronic shortages in high-demand zones.

AI Solution:

- Deployed a multi-echelon AI engine to reposition stock dynamically

- Used real-time POS data, weather signals, and fashion trend models

- Integrated with the replenishment system for daily automatic orders

Results:

- 35% reduction in stockouts

- Inventory value reduced by $8.7M

- Store-level sell-through improved by 21%

- DC inventory turns increased from 5.2 to 10.3

Case Study: Industrial MRO Spare Parts

Challenge:
A mining company held over 150,000 SKUs of critical spare parts with no clear demand patterns. Carrying costs were extreme, and emergency procurement delays cost millions.

AI Solution:

- Implemented a demand classification model (intermittent, cyclical, lumpy)

- Used clustering to identify pooling opportunities across sites

- Applied probabilistic reorder modeling with part criticality scores

Results:

- Inventory value reduced by 18%

- Emergency procurement events down 47%

- Service level maintained at 99.2%

- Identified $3.4M in obsolete stock write-offs

AI-Driven Inventory Levers

1. **Dynamic Safety Stock:**
   Continuously adjusts buffers based on demand variability, supplier performance, and lead time risk.

2. **Automated Replenishment Triggers:**
   AI recalculates reorder points daily using updated data.

3. **Strategic Inventory Placement:**
   Optimizes where to hold stock—central vs. regional DCs vs. in-store—based on cost-to-serve and lead time.

4. **Lifecycle-Aware Planning:**
   Forecasts ramp-up, peak, and decline phases to prevent overbuying late in product life.

5. **Backorder vs. Expedite Optimization:**
   Decides when to wait vs. when to air-ship, based on customer value and margin impact.

Best Practices for Implementation

- **Clean Your Master Data:**
  Ensure SKUs, units of measure, and location hierarchies are accurate.

- **Start with High-Impact Categories:**
  Focus on top 20% SKUs by value, margin, or volume.

- **Integrate With WMS and ERP:**
  Ensure AI signals feed directly into replenishment, transfer, and purchasing workflows.

- **Build Inventory Visibility First:**
  Track stock in transit, returns, and shelf-level depletion before optimizing policies.

- **Establish Service-Level Targets:**
  Align AI goals with business objectives—whether that's cash preservation, growth, or customer experience.

Summary

Inventory optimization powered by AI turns guesswork into precision. It replaces blunt rules with **fine-tuned, adaptive models** that continuously balance supply, demand, cost, and risk across the network.

Whether you're managing raw materials, finished goods, or slow-moving spares, AI helps you stock smarter—not just more.

In the next section, we'll explore how AI transforms **logistics and transportation planning**—ensuring inventory gets where it needs to go, as fast and efficiently as possible.

5.4 AI in Logistics and Transportation Optimization

In the world of supply chains, logistics is where plans meet pavement. It's the movement of goods from suppliers to factories, warehouses to stores, and fulfillment centers to customers. And it's one of the most complex, costly, and carbon-intensive components of operations.

With surging e-commerce volumes, fuel volatility, labor shortages, and sustainability demands, logistics is under more pressure than ever. AI steps in to **orchestrate every mile with intelligence—reducing cost, improving on-time delivery, and making routes adaptive in real time**.

Logistics Complexity Today

Modern logistics operations juggle thousands of variables:

- Multiple carriers, lanes, and service levels

- Varying truck capacities and constraints

- Delivery windows and customer SLAs

- Weather, traffic, and border delays

- Volatile fuel and toll pricing

- Regulatory limits on driver hours

- Carbon footprint reduction goals

Managing all of this manually—or with static TMS rules—is no longer feasible. AI enables optimization across the full chain of logistics—from **route planning to fleet management, freight procurement to last-mile orchestration**.

Key Applications of AI in Logistics

1. Route and Load Optimization

AI analyzes delivery points, vehicle capacities, driver shifts, and traffic data to determine the most efficient routes and loads—reducing miles, fuel, and delivery time.

Technologies Used:

- Heuristic and metaheuristic algorithms (e.g., Ant Colony, Tabu Search)

- Constraint-based optimization for time windows, vehicle types, delivery priority

- Predictive traffic and weather integration

Impact:
Reduces route costs by 10–25%, with higher on-time delivery.

2. Dynamic Delivery Scheduling

AI adjusts delivery times dynamically based on:

- Customer availability

- Driver ETAs

- Inventory readiness

- Real-time road conditions

Example:
An AI scheduler may reschedule a delivery to a hospital an hour earlier if it predicts a traffic slowdown later in the day, maximizing on-time fulfillment.

3. Predictive ETA and Delay Management

AI models use historical and real-time data to predict delivery times more accurately than traditional GPS systems.

Data Inputs:

- Traffic feeds and road closures

- Driver behavior and past performance

- Warehouse readiness and dwell time

- Port or border clearance delays

Outcome:
More reliable ETAs, better customer communication, fewer "where is my order" calls.

4. Freight Procurement and Carrier Selection

AI matches loads to carriers dynamically, using:

- Price prediction models

- Carrier performance scoring

- Availability forecasting

- Lane consolidation opportunities

Impact:
Reduces reliance on spot markets and improves rate consistency.

5. Warehouse-to-Transport Coordination

AI synchronizes outbound shipments with warehouse readiness:

- Schedules pick/pack sequences aligned to truck arrival

- Balances dock utilization and reduces wait times

- Dynamically reroutes loads from full DCs to alternate sites

Example:
A global electronics firm uses AI to direct trucks to DCs with excess capacity, cutting turnaround time by 28%.

6. Last-Mile Delivery Optimization

For direct-to-consumer models, AI personalizes
and automates the final mile:

- Smart delivery window recommendations

- Route clustering by location, product
  type, and vehicle size

- Driver routing apps with live update
  instructions

- Customer communication bots for delay
  alerts and rescheduling

Impact:
Boosts customer satisfaction and minimizes
failed delivery attempts.

Case Study: AI in Retail Delivery Routing

Challenge:
A large grocery chain delivering from regional DCs to 600+ stores faced rising transport costs and inconsistent delivery timing.

AI Solution:

- Used a hybrid routing engine with reinforcement learning to simulate route sequences

- Integrated fuel price data and driver shift rules

- Scheduled loads to optimize vehicle fill while preserving shelf-life priorities

Results:

- Cost per route reduced by 18%

- On-time deliveries improved from 85% to 96%

- Weekly route planning time cut from 14 hours to under 1

Case Study: Manufacturing Logistics Control Tower

Challenge:
A heavy machinery company needed to coordinate global inbound parts shipments from 150+ suppliers via ocean, air, and road modes.

AI Solution:

- Implemented a logistics control tower powered by AI to track, simulate, and replan shipments

- Used weather and port delay prediction models to suggest rerouting

- Automated mode shifts (e.g., ocean to air) based on part criticality and factory needs

- **Results:**
- 43% fewer factory stoppages from parts unavailability

- Average lead time variance cut by 21%

- On-time inbound performance reached 97.5%

Benefits of AI in Logistics

Benefit	Result
Reduced Mileage	10–30% savings through route optimization
Lower Fuel Costs	Real-time adaptation and eco-routing
Improved On-Time Delivery	Predictive ETAs and dynamic rescheduling
Higher Vehicle Utilization	Smarter load planning and zone bundling
Better Customer Experience	Proactive alerts and personalized delivery
Lower Emissions	Green routing and carbon-aware scheduling

Implementation Best Practices

1. **Start with One Region or Lane:**
   Run AI logistics in parallel with legacy routing to measure the lift.

2. **Feed the Right Data:**
   Integrate TMS, GPS, WMS, weather, and telematics data.

3. **Make It Human-Friendly:**
   Dispatchers and drivers must trust and understand the AI's decisions.

4. **Automate Exceptions Gradually:**
   Begin with route planning, then expand to freight tendering, load rebalancing, and last-mile notifications.

5. **Measure and Report:**
   Track delivery KPIs, cost per mile, CO_2 per delivery, and SLA adherence.

Summary

AI turns logistics from a reactive, rules-based operation into a **live, intelligent system**—continuously optimizing how goods move, where delays occur, and what decisions reduce cost without sacrificing service.

Whether you're managing global freight, regional distribution, or last-mile customer delivery, AI makes every shipment smarter, faster, and greener.

In the next section, we'll explore how AI addresses **supply chain risk and resilience**, preparing your network to survive and thrive amid constant uncertainty.

5.5 AI for Risk Management and Supply Chain Resilience

Resilience has become the new currency of supply chain excellence. Once a background concern, supply chain risk is now front and center—driven by pandemics, wars, cyberattacks, climate events, and raw material shortages. Manufacturers can no longer afford to simply react to disruptions—they must **anticipate, simulate, and act ahead of time**.

Artificial intelligence provides the foundation for this transformation. It enables supply chains to shift from brittle to adaptive, from opaque to transparent, from vulnerable to intelligent.

The Nature of Supply Chain Risk Today

Supply chain risk comes in many forms:

- **Operational:** Equipment failures, inventory misallocations, labor strikes

- **Supplier-related:** Insolvency, capacity issues, quality failures

- **Geopolitical:** Trade restrictions, sanctions, political instability

- **Environmental:** Earthquakes, floods, wildfires, and weather events

- **Cyber:** Data breaches, ransomware attacks on logistics or ERP systems

- **Financial:** Currency volatility, fuel cost spikes, interest rate shifts

- **Compliance & ESG:** Human rights violations, regulatory audits, emissions reporting gaps

Most of these risks are interrelated, hard to detect early, and difficult to quantify with traditional methods.

How AI Enables Resilient Supply Chains

AI brings a new toolkit to supply chain risk management:

- **Prediction:** Forecasting disruption likelihood based on patterns and signals

- **Detection:** Real-time monitoring of news, sensor feeds, and vendor performance

- **Simulation:** Modeling what-if scenarios across sourcing, inventory, and logistics

- **Prescriptive Action:** Recommending mitigation steps—alternate suppliers, stock reallocation, rerouting

- **Learning:** Improving future response through reinforcement and feedback

Together, these capabilities create **self-healing supply chains** that don't just survive uncertainty—they adapt through it.

Key AI Applications in Risk Management

1. Supplier Risk Scoring

- Uses ML models to assess suppliers based on financials, performance, geography, ESG, and news sentiment

- Tracks late shipments, quality issues, credit ratings, litigation, and natural hazard exposure

Example:
 A pharma company receives early alerts when a Tier 2 raw material supplier in China is hit by flooding—triggering a preemptive switch to an alternate source.

2. Disruption Detection via NLP and External Signals

- AI scans global news, social media, port updates, weather alerts, and government advisories

- Uses NLP to extract risk-relevant events (e.g., strike threats, unrest, cyberattacks)

Example:
A CPG company uses AI to track geopolitical tension in a key palm oil-producing region—activating risk assessments and scenario planning 6 weeks ahead of competitors.

3. Multi-Tier Network Visibility

- AI helps map not just direct suppliers but indirect ones—Tier 2 and 3 vendors

- Detects vulnerabilities in sub-tier nodes (e.g., single-source materials, shared transport hubs)

Use Case:
An automaker uses AI to discover that multiple Tier 1 suppliers rely on the same Tier 3 semiconductor plant in Taiwan—diversifying sourcing before shortages hit.

---

4. Predictive Inventory Buffering

- Uses simulation and Monte Carlo modeling to forecast stockout probabilities based on supply chain shocks

- Dynamically adjusts buffer stock, safety levels, and allocation priorities

Impact:
Prevents overreaction and panic buying while improving service levels under uncertainty.

---

5. Scenario Simulation and Decision Support

- Models "what-if" events like factory shutdowns, port closures, or demand surges

- Quantifies impact on revenue, lead time, cost, and emissions

- Suggests mitigation tactics (e.g., expedited freight, dual sourcing, production shifting)

Example:
A heavy equipment manufacturer models the impact of steel price volatility and shifts sourcing contracts from monthly to index-linked hedges.

6. Autonomous Risk Playbooks

- AI engines activate predefined contingency plans when disruption signals cross thresholds

- Automates responses like supplier notification, inventory reallocation, and logistics rerouting

Result:
Faster, more consistent, and lower-error disruption response—even across complex networks.

Benefits of AI-Driven Resilience

Dimension	Traditional Supply Chain	AI-Augmented Supply Chain
Disruption Detection	Reactive, manual	Predictive, real-time
Supplier Visibility	Tier 1 only	Full multi-tier insights
Scenario Planning	Spreadsheet-based	Automated, multi-variable
Decision Speed	Days to weeks	Minutes to hours
Response Quality	Variable, tribal knowledge	Consistent, data-driven
Adaptability	Rigid and slow	Self-correcting and dynamic

Case Study: Aerospace Component Manufacturer

Challenge:
Highly specialized parts sourced from niche suppliers created single points of failure. A volcanic eruption halted air freight from a key supplier region.

AI Solution:

- Risk engine predicted growing ash cloud disruption 4 days in advance

- Modeled alternate part sourcing and route options

- Activated preapproved supplier contracts in Europe and rerouted via rail

Results:

- Zero disruption to production lines

- Avoided over $4.5M in downtime penalties

- Gained board-level support to roll out AI across all sourcing categories

Implementation Steps

1. **Map Your Network**
   Use AI tools to discover your full supplier ecosystem—including sub-tiers.

2. **Identify Critical Nodes**
   Prioritize risk models around high-impact suppliers, lanes, and facilities.

3. **Feed External Signals**
   Integrate live data: weather, news, social, economic indicators.

4. **Create Playbooks**
   Define AI triggers and preapproved actions for various disruption types.

5. **Align Governance**
   Ensure legal, procurement, and ops teams are involved in AI risk workflows.

Summary

AI doesn't eliminate risk—but it enables manufacturers to face it with foresight and flexibility. By combining early warning systems with simulation and automation, AI makes **resilience measurable, repeatable, and scalable**.

In a world where the next crisis is always just one headline away, **intelligent risk management isn't optional—it's operational armor.**

Next, we'll wrap up this chapter with a conclusion summarizing the end-to-end impact of AI across the supply chain.

Conclusion: The Intelligent Supply Chain

The traditional supply chain was designed for stability, scale, and repetition. It worked well in a world where demand patterns were predictable, borders stayed open, and suppliers were close by. But that world is gone.

Today, manufacturers face a reality where volatility is the norm. From geopolitical unrest and raw material shortages to consumer unpredictability and climate disruptions, the old supply chain playbook can no longer keep pace.

Artificial intelligence rewrites that playbook—enabling a new era of visibility, agility, and resilience.

What We've Learned

This chapter explored how AI transforms every layer of the supply chain into a smarter, faster, and more responsive system:

- **Forecasting & Demand Sensing:** AI replaces static projections with dynamic, multi-signal predictions—improving accuracy and reducing stockouts.

- **Procurement & Supplier Optimization:** Machine learning automates sourcing, monitors vendor health, and enables strategic diversification before disruptions hit.

- **Inventory Optimization:** Adaptive policies ensure the right stock, in the right place, at the right time—minimizing waste while maximizing service levels.

- **Logistics & Transportation:** AI orchestrates freight with live routing, load optimization, and predictive ETA management—lowering costs and carbon footprints.

- **Risk & Resilience:**
  AI senses disruption early, simulates impact, and activates response playbooks—building self-healing, self-correcting networks.

Together, these capabilities form the **intelligent supply chain**: a living system that **learns from the past, senses the present, and prepares for the future**—in real time.

Strategic Impact

Dimension	Old Supply Chain	AI-Driven Supply Chain
Forecasting	Historical averages	Signal fusion & real-time models
Sourcing	Cost-focused	Risk- and resilience-informed
Inventory	Rule-based buffers	Predictive and adaptive
Logistics	Fixed routes & schedules	Live optimization and re-routing
Disruption Response	Reactive firefighting	Proactive, automated action
Decision Speed	Weeks	Minutes

By embracing AI, manufacturers can lower costs, improve customer experience, reduce emissions,

and gain a lasting edge over competitors still
clinging to manual, reactive methods.

A Roadmap for Leaders

To build an intelligent supply chain, begin with these steps:

1. **Establish a Data Foundation**
   Clean, unify, and connect your planning, execution, and partner data.

2. **Pilot High-Impact Use Cases**
   Start with forecasting, inventory, or routing—where results are visible and measurable.

3. **Invest in Cross-Functional AI Fluency**
   Train teams across procurement, logistics, and finance to understand and trust AI outputs.

4. **Prioritize Visibility and Resilience**
   Extend visibility beyond Tier 1 suppliers and model risk proactively.

5. **Build AI into Daily Decisions**
   Integrate AI insights into the workflows of planners, buyers, and dispatchers—not just dashboards.

Looking Forward

The intelligent supply chain is not a single technology or tool—it's a strategic shift. A move away from control through rigidity, and toward agility through intelligence. A move from static planning to adaptive execution. A move from surviving disruptions to anticipating them.

In the next chapter, we zoom in on the factory floor—exploring how AI is reshaping **operations, robotics, and real-time control systems** to deliver Industry 4.0 in full force.

Because a smart supply chain is only as strong as the intelligence inside the plant.

6.0 Introduction: Intelligence in Motion

The factory floor has always been where value is created. It's the site of motion, assembly, transformation—where raw materials become finished goods. But for decades, even the most advanced factories relied on rigid logic, fixed automation, and human oversight to make everything work.

Now, artificial intelligence is bringing the next revolution: **factories that think, learn, and adapt in real time.**

AI doesn't just live in the cloud or office analytics dashboards—it's increasingly embedded in machines, sensors, vision systems, controllers, and collaborative robots (cobots) on the shop floor. It enables systems to monitor, analyze, and optimize their own performance—reducing errors, minimizing downtime, and augmenting human potential.

This is not just automation—it's **intelligence in motion.**

The Old Paradigm: Fixed Logic, Fragile Flexibility

Traditional factory systems relied on:

- Hardcoded PLC rules

- Preset tolerances and alerts

- Batch updates from MES or ERP systems

- Human-led troubleshooting

- Visual checks and manual data collection

These systems were powerful, but also brittle. A slight change in material behavior, product spec, or environmental condition could lead to waste, rework, or line stoppages.

The more complex the product, the higher the variability, the more costly the inflexibility.

The AI-Enabled Factory

With artificial intelligence, the factory floor becomes a **sensing, learning, and decision-making environment**. AI:

- **Recognizes patterns** across process variables, quality, and machine behavior

- **Learns from historical data** to predict failures and adjust settings

- **Interprets visual inputs** to detect defects, misalignment, or foreign objects

- **Coordinates robots and workers** based on task complexity and safety

- **Continuously improves** by ingesting feedback from every cycle

In short, AI closes the loop between **perception, decision, and action.**

Core Domains of AI on the Factory Floor

In this chapter, we'll explore the key areas where AI is driving transformation in operations:

1. **Predictive Maintenance:**
   Anticipating machine failures before they happen using vibration, temperature, current, and audio data.

2. **Process Optimization:**
   Adjusting setpoints, flow rates, temperatures, or speeds in real time for yield, energy, or quality improvement.

3. **Computer Vision & Quality Control:**
   Detecting defects, verifying assembly, guiding robots, and replacing manual visual inspection.

4. **Cobotics and Human-AI Collaboration:**
   AI-enabled robots that work safely alongside humans—learning from motion data and contextual cues.

5. **Autonomous Material Handling:**
   AGVs, AMRs, and drones powered by AI-based navigation and demand signals.

6. **Production Monitoring & Digital Twins:**
   Real-time simulation and control using
   AI-trained digital replicas of processes or
   entire lines.

Why It Matters Now

AI brings new possibilities to manufacturing operations:

- **Greater uptime** through condition-based and predictive maintenance

- **Higher first-pass yield** via smarter process adjustments

- **Faster problem-solving** with AI-assisted root cause analysis

- **Enhanced flexibility** in high-mix or customized environments

- **Real-time adaptation** to changing inputs, demand, or operator availability

In a time where customer expectations are rising and labor is scarce, AI enables manufacturers to **do more with less—better, faster, and smarter.**

Chapter Preview

In the sections ahead, we'll explore:

- How predictive maintenance systems are built and deployed

- The use of reinforcement learning to fine-tune process parameters

- Computer vision models that surpass human inspectors

- Cobot platforms and safety frameworks

- Use cases of AI-enabled real-time control and digital twins

With real-world case studies and implementation insights, this chapter shows how AI isn't just supporting factory operations—it's **transforming the very nature of work, machines, and performance.**

6.1 Predictive Maintenance and Equipment Intelligence

In traditional manufacturing, maintenance has often been a balancing act: too little, and you risk catastrophic failures; too much, and you waste time, money, and resources. Preventive schedules based on runtime or calendar dates helped, but they were blunt tools—treating all machines equally, regardless of actual wear or risk.

Artificial intelligence changes this equation completely. With predictive maintenance (PdM), AI empowers factories to **see inside machines, understand their behavior, and act before failure occurs**.

The Limitations of Preventive and Reactive Maintenance

Type	Description	Limitation
Reactive	Fix after failure	High cost, unplanned downtime
Preventive	Scheduled based on time/cycles	Wasteful, may miss early failure signs
Predictive (AI)	Monitor real-time conditions, forecast failure	Precise, data-driven, cost-effective

Reactive and preventive models often rely on tribal knowledge, static rules, or OEM recommendations—missing early-stage anomalies and treating every asset the same. AI flips the model, tailoring decisions to **the individual health of each machine**.

What Is Predictive Maintenance?

Predictive maintenance uses AI and machine learning models to:

- Monitor machine health in real time

- Detect abnormal patterns in operation

- Predict time to failure with confidence intervals

- Recommend interventions (e.g., lubrication, alignment, part replacement)

- Minimize unplanned downtime and extend asset life

It's like giving your machines a sixth sense—and giving your maintenance team a crystal ball.

Core Technologies Enabling Predictive Maintenance

1. IoT Sensors and Edge Devices

- Vibration sensors (accelerometers)

- Acoustic sensors (ultrasound, microphones)

- Temperature, humidity, and pressure sensors

- Current, voltage, and power draw monitors

- Edge AI devices for local data processing

2. Data Acquisition and Condition Monitoring

- SCADA systems and historian databases

- Time-series data collection at high frequency

- Labeling failure events, wear patterns, and operational anomalies

3. **Machine Learning Algorithms**

- Anomaly detection using unsupervised learning (e.g., autoencoders, isolation forests)

- Supervised models (e.g., random forests, SVMs) trained on failure history

- Predictive regression (e.g., remaining useful life (RUL) estimation)

- Deep learning for complex, multivariate sensor fusion

4. **Dashboards and Alerting Systems**

- Maintenance dashboards with asset health scores

- Predictive alerts with lead time recommendations

- Integration with CMMS (Computerized Maintenance Management System)

Benefits of AI-Based Maintenance

Benefit	Impact
Reduced Unplanned Downtime	30–70% reduction
Extended Asset Life	Optimized replacement schedules
Lower Maintenance Costs	Fewer unnecessary checks or replacements
Improved Safety	Avoids catastrophic failures
Higher OEE (Overall Equipment Effectiveness)	Better uptime, performance, and quality

Case Study: Automotive Engine Plant

Challenge:
An engine assembly line experienced frequent unplanned stoppages due to bearing failures in critical conveyors.

AI Solution:

- Deployed vibration and acoustic sensors on key rollers

- Trained ML model to detect deviation from normal vibration profiles

- Used predictive alerts with RUL estimates

Results:

- Unplanned downtime reduced by 58%

- Bearing replacement scheduled during regular shift windows

- Saved $870,000 in downtime and overtime within one year

Case Study: Food & Beverage Facility

Challenge:
A bottling line suffered intermittent jams in high-speed labeling equipment, causing cascading delays.

AI Solution:

- Anomaly detection using audio and motor torque data

- Edge AI device analyzed signals locally and sent alerts to operators

- Integrated with visual inspection to confirm mechanical wear

Results:

- MTBF (mean time between failures) improved by 3.2x

- False alarms decreased by 47%

- Maintenance workload rebalanced toward high-value tasks

Predictive Maintenance Deployment Process

1. **Identify Critical Assets**
   Focus on equipment with high repair cost, long lead time, or impact on throughput.

2. **Instrument with Sensors**
   Choose appropriate sensors (vibration, acoustic, temperature) and install near failure-prone components.

3. **Collect Baseline Data**
   Monitor healthy behavior to train AI on "normal" signatures.

4. **Label Failures and Events**
   Tag data around known issues to teach the model failure characteristics.

5. **Train and Test Models**
   Use historical and live data to build prediction engines, validating accuracy and false positive rates.

6. **Deploy with Alerts and CMMS Integration**
   Set thresholds, delivery channels (email/SMS), and link alerts to work

orders.

7. **Iterate and Retrain**
Continuously refine models with new failures, seasonal shifts, and process changes.

Challenges and Considerations

- **Data Quality:** Garbage in, garbage out. Sensor noise, signal loss, and incorrect labeling can derail models.

- **ROI Visibility:** Start with a focused pilot to demonstrate clear cost avoidance.

- **Change Management:** Operators and technicians must trust and act on AI-generated insights.

- **Integration Needs:** Connect PdM systems to ERP, MES, and CMMS for seamless execution.

- **Cybersecurity:** Protect industrial IoT devices from unauthorized access or tampering.

Summary

AI-based predictive maintenance transforms maintenance from a cost center to a strategic advantage. It reduces downtime, improves safety, optimizes inventory of spares, and frees technicians to focus on high-impact tasks.

Instead of waiting for machines to break—or replacing parts "just in case"—factories can now **maintain exactly when it's needed, and never more.**

In the next section, we'll explore how AI goes beyond equipment health to **optimize production processes in real time**—increasing yield, reducing waste, and elevating efficiency to new heights.

6.2 Real-Time Process Optimization with AI

Manufacturing success hinges not only on keeping machines running—but on keeping them running **at their best**. Every process—whether it's mixing, molding, welding, or coating—has dozens of parameters that affect throughput, quality, cost, and energy use.

Traditionally, optimizing these parameters involved static rules, expert intuition, and slow trial-and-error. But with AI, manufacturers can now continuously monitor process variables and **automatically adjust settings in real time** to improve output and reduce waste.

This is not just automation—it's **adaptive control based on learning**, turning every production cycle into a data-driven opportunity for improvement.

The Need for Dynamic Optimization

Manufacturing environments are rarely stable. Variability can arise from:

- Raw material inconsistencies

- Ambient temperature or humidity changes

- Wear and tear on equipment

- Operator differences

- Shift-to-shift drift in process setup

Even small deviations can lead to:

- Lower yields

- Quality defects

- Higher energy or material consumption

- Unplanned downtime

AI enables a smarter response: detecting drift early, understanding its cause, and tuning process settings to maintain optimal output.

Core Technologies in Real-Time Process Optimization

1. Advanced Process Control (APC) Enhanced by AI

- Traditional APC uses control loops (PID, MPC) to maintain stability.

- AI augments APC with learning from historical and real-time data to fine-tune parameters proactively.

2. Machine Learning-Based Setpoint Adjustment

- Regression models or neural networks learn relationships between inputs (e.g., temperature, pressure, flow) and outputs (e.g., defect rate, yield).

- Models then recommend or automatically apply optimal setpoints based on live sensor readings.

3. Reinforcement Learning (RL)

- AI agents explore process conditions and "learn by doing" over thousands of cycles.

- The system receives feedback (reward signals) for achieving goals like lower energy use or better throughput.

- RL adapts to shifting environments, making it ideal for high-mix or variable processes.

4. Digital Twins

- AI models replicate the behavior of a physical process in a virtual environment.

- Real-time inputs are fed into the twin, which tests multiple scenarios before applying the best one on the real line.

- Helps validate changes safely and quickly.

Benefits of AI-Driven Optimization

Benefit	Impact
Higher Yield	Reduce scrap, rework, and missed targets
Lower Cost per Unit	Optimize cycle time, energy, and inputs
Improved Consistency	Reduce variance across shifts or batches
Faster Ramp-Up	Quicker setup for new SKUs or products
Fewer Manual Interventions	Operators focus on value-add tasks

Case Study: Chemical Coatings Line

Challenge:
A coatings line suffered from batch-to-batch variability in viscosity, affecting surface finish and requiring frequent manual tuning.

AI Solution:

- Used ML models to predict viscosity outcomes based on process temperature, solvent ratio, and mixer speed.

- System recommended setpoint changes every 10 minutes based on predicted variance.

- Integrated with SCADA to execute approved adjustments automatically.

Results:

- Product consistency improved by 24%

- Scrap volume cut by 31%

- Operator interventions reduced by 60%

- $1.2M annual savings in raw material and rework costs

Case Study: Injection Molding Optimization

Challenge:
A plastic injection molding facility faced frequent part rejects due to flash and warpage during weather changes.

AI Solution:

- Trained a reinforcement learning agent to tune mold temperature, injection speed, and cooling time.

- Used part quality data from 3D scanners to provide feedback.

- Adapted in real time based on shop floor conditions.

  Results:

- First-pass yield increased from 82% to 96%

- Energy use per part dropped 18%

- Changeover time for new molds cut by 35%

Implementation Roadmap

1. **Select a Stable Process with Optimization Potential**
   Ideal candidates have measurable KPIs (e.g., yield, cost, defect rate) and sufficient variability to improve.

2. **Instrument the Process with Sensors**
   Capture key input/output variables in real time.

3. **Build Historical Dataset**
   Train ML models on existing process data to learn input-output relationships.

4. **Choose Optimization Framework**
   For deterministic systems: regression or neural networks.
   For dynamic/variable systems: reinforcement learning or digital twins.

5. **Deploy in Supervised Mode First**
   Let AI suggest changes, but have human operators approve them.

6. **Move to Autonomous Control**
   Once models are validated, integrate with PLCs, DCS, or SCADA for real-time

adjustment.

7. **Measure and Improve**
   Track KPI improvement, model drift, and
   retrain periodically.

Challenges and Mitigations

- **Model Drift:** Processes evolve—retrain
  models regularly using new data.

- **Operator Resistance:** Involve
  technicians early, explain AI decisions
  clearly.

- **Safety Constraints:** Set strict bounds on
  allowable AI adjustments to avoid unsafe
  states.

- **Integration Complexity:** Work with
  control engineers to align AI with existing
  automation logic.

Summary

AI-driven process optimization brings the vision of self-improving factories to life. Instead of setting parameters once and hoping for the best, manufacturers can now **continuously adapt**—every cycle, every shift, every day.

In the next section, we'll explore how **AI and computer vision** work together to automate quality inspection, guide robots, and provide new levels of visual intelligence on the shop floor.

6.3 Computer Vision and Intelligent Inspection

The human eye has long been the standard for factory inspection—capable, flexible, and surprisingly adaptive. But it's also limited. Fatigue sets in. Tiny variations are missed. Inconsistent decisions creep in across shifts. And the sheer scale of modern manufacturing makes 100% inspection nearly impossible by manual means.

Enter **AI-powered computer vision**—a technology that mimics and exceeds the capabilities of human visual inspection, delivering speed, precision, and scalability that transforms quality control and operational awareness.

From detecting surface defects to guiding robotic arms, computer vision is turning every camera into a smart sensor—and every image into actionable insight.

The Limitations of Traditional Visual Inspection

Manual inspection, even with standard cameras and rule-based algorithms, struggles with:

- Subtle or rare defect types

- Changing lighting or surface conditions

- Subjective decision-making across operators

- Inability to scale across multiple lines or locations

- High labor costs and inspection fatigue

Conventional vision systems, based on static thresholding or geometric rules, often break down when variability increases. They require frequent reprogramming and struggle with complex textures, materials, or object deformations.

AI vision systems overcome these issues by **learning patterns**, recognizing context, and adapting to visual diversity.

What Is AI-Powered Computer Vision?

Computer vision powered by artificial intelligence uses **deep learning models**, typically convolutional neural networks (CNNs), to interpret images and video. These models can:

- Detect surface defects (scratches, dents, holes, smudges)

- Classify parts or assemblies

- Verify alignment, positioning, or completeness

- Detect anomalies not seen during training

- Track objects or people in motion

- Guide robotic arms using visual cues

Unlike rule-based logic, AI vision systems **learn from labeled data** and improve over time.

Key Applications on the Factory Floor

1. Defect Detection

AI models analyze images of components, surfaces, or assemblies to spot:

- Cracks, chips, or pitting

- Color inconsistencies

- Weld flaws or incomplete joints

- Label misprints or misalignments

- Fiber or grain anomalies (e.g., in textiles or wood)

Benefits:

- 24/7 operation with consistent performance

- Higher defect detection rates (especially for rare cases)

- Ability to handle variation in part shape, color, or texture

---

2. Assembly Verification

AI ensures that parts are:

- Correctly oriented and placed

- Fully assembled with all subcomponents

- Free from missing bolts, seals, or labels

- Within positional tolerances

This is critical in high-mix assembly lines (e.g., electronics, automotive dashboards).

---

3. Robot Guidance (Vision-Guided Robotics)

Cameras equipped with AI detect:

- Part location and orientation

- Bin picking patterns (for random parts in containers)

- Safety zones for cobot collaboration

- Part variation for adaptive grip strategies

Impact:
Reduces reliance on precision fixturing, enabling greater flexibility.

---

4. Safety and Compliance Monitoring

AI vision can track:

- Whether operators wear PPE (gloves, helmets, goggles)

- Entry into restricted areas

- Unsafe posture or proximity to moving machinery

- Fire, smoke, or spill detection

Helps ensure safety protocols are followed—and alerts are issued before incidents occur.

5. Real-Time Data Logging and Traceability

AI vision systems can:

- Save defect images with timestamps and product IDs

- Create digital quality logs for every item

- Enable root cause analysis through visual evidence

- Facilitate regulatory compliance and warranty traceability

Case Study: Electronics PCB Inspection

Challenge:
Manual and rule-based vision inspection missed fine soldering defects and struggled with new board layouts.

AI Solution:

- Trained a CNN on thousands of labeled PCB images across product variants

- Detected solder bridges, tombstoning, and missing components

- Deployed on edge devices for instant inspection at 120 boards/minute

Results:

- False negatives reduced by 63%

- Rework rate cut by 47%

- Inspection headcount reduced from 5 to 1 per shift

Case Study: Automotive Paint Shop

Challenge:
High-end car finishes showed microdefects that escaped human inspection, especially under variable lighting.

AI Solution:

- Installed high-resolution line-scan cameras and trained defect classification models

- Integrated lighting control and defect annotation tools for inspectors to refine models

- Enabled feedback loop to adjust painting process settings

Results:

- Detection accuracy improved by 72%

- Downtime due to repainting reduced by 38%

- Operator satisfaction increased due to reduced error disputes

Implementation Guide

1. **Choose the Right Use Case**
   Start with a visual task that's frequent, costly to miss, and hard to inspect manually.

2. **Gather High-Quality Image Data**
   Use consistent lighting, varied examples, and expert-labeled defects.

3. **Train and Validate AI Models**
   Begin with classification, then move to segmentation or object detection as needed.

4. **Integrate with Production Systems**
   Deploy on edge devices or cloud with links to MES, quality logs, or PLCs.

5. **Enable Human Feedback Loops**
   Let operators flag false positives or new defect types to retrain models.

Challenges and Solutions

- **Data Labeling Effort:** Mitigated by semi-supervised learning and synthetic data generation.

- **Model Drift:** Retrain periodically as lighting, materials, or designs change.

- **Edge vs. Cloud Processing:** Use edge AI for real-time response; cloud for training and analysis.

- **Operator Buy-In:** Demonstrate how AI aids—not replaces—their expertise.

Summary

AI-powered computer vision upgrades the eyes of your factory—making inspection faster, smarter, and more scalable. It doesn't just replace human vision—it **amplifies it**, ensuring every product meets spec, every defect is documented, and every opportunity for improvement is visible.

In the next section, we'll explore how AI brings intelligence to human-robot collaboration—creating flexible, safe, and productive workspaces where humans and machines learn together.

6.4 Collaborative Robotics and Human-AI Interaction

The factory of the future is not fully human. Nor is it fully robotic. It is **collaborative**—a space where human expertise and robotic precision coexist, complement, and co-evolve. At the heart of this partnership is **artificial intelligence**, making machines not just programmable, but context-aware and cooperative.

Collaborative robots—or **cobots**—are reshaping how work gets done on the shop floor. When powered by AI, these systems can **sense, adapt, and learn from humans in real time**, creating work environments that are safer, smarter, and more efficient.

Why Collaboration Matters

Industrial robots have long delivered speed, strength, and repeatability—but they traditionally required:

- Heavy cages and safety barriers

- Pre-programmed paths

- Dedicated space and tasks

- Skilled programmers to make changes

This rigidity limited their use in high-mix, low-volume environments and tasks requiring human judgment or dexterity.

AI-enabled cobots, in contrast, are designed to:

- Share workspaces with people safely

- Adjust their actions based on human motion or verbal cues

- Learn new tasks through demonstration

- Switch between tasks with minimal reprogramming

The result is a new division of labor—where robots handle the repetitive, dangerous, or heavy lifting, while humans oversee quality, make decisions, and adapt on the fly.

AI Capabilities in Collaborative Robotics

1. Vision and Perception

- AI-powered cameras and 3D sensors help cobots identify objects, track human positions, and recognize gestures or tools.

- Deep learning models detect part orientation, color variations, or workspace layout changes.

2. Motion Planning and Prediction

- Machine learning enables smooth, dynamic path planning.

- AI anticipates human motion, avoiding collisions or adapting routes in real time.

3. Force and Tactile Feedback

- Cobots with AI-tuned force sensors can detect contact pressure and adjust grip or movement accordingly.

- Enables delicate tasks like assembly, packaging, or polishing.

4. Voice and Gesture Interfaces

- Natural language processing allows workers to instruct robots using voice commands.

- Gesture recognition models support intuitive communication (e.g., pointing, waving, thumbs up).

5. Learning from Demonstration (LfD)

- AI enables cobots to observe and replicate human-performed tasks.

- Reduces the need for complex coding and accelerates deployment in dynamic environments.

Common Use Cases for AI Cobots

Task	Application Examples
Assembly Assistance	Screwing, inserting, positioning parts
Material Handling	Loading/unloading machines, palletizing
Packaging and Sorting	Visual inspection, bin packing, boxing
Finishing Tasks	Polishing, sanding, deburring
Quality Inspection	Camera-guided defect identification
Tool Handoff	Passing tools to humans during complex tasks

Case Study: Appliance Manufacturing

Challenge:
Manual screwdriving tasks on mixed-model lines caused repetitive strain injuries and inconsistencies across shifts.

AI Solution:

- Deployed cobots with vision and torque control to assist in screwdriving.

- Cobots learned locations through demonstration and verified placement with vision.

- Human operators focused on part placement and visual verification.

Results:

- Injury risk reduced by 78%

- Assembly cycle time cut by 22%

- Operator satisfaction improved due to reduced strain and task monotony

Case Study: Automotive Final Assembly

Challenge:
Assembly lines required fast changeovers and collaboration between workers and machines in tight spaces.

AI Solution:

- Cobots were equipped with 360° vision, adaptive path planning, and voice feedback.

- AI ensured cobots paused, slowed, or rerouted when humans entered proximity.

- Enabled mixed-model production without stopping the line.

Results:

- Changeover time reduced by 40%

- Robot incidents dropped to near zero

- Flexibility enabled production of 3 car models on one line

Human Factors and Safety Considerations

- **ISO 10218 and ISO/TS 15066** define standards for safe human-robot collaboration.

- AI systems must monitor force, speed, and proximity at all times.

- Emergency stop and override mechanisms should always be accessible.

- Clear visual and auditory signals reduce cognitive overload and improve trust.

Trust is key: Operators must feel confident that cobots will behave predictably and respectfully in shared spaces.

Best Practices for Deployment

1. **Select Tasks with a Clear ROI**
   Focus on repetitive, ergonomic, or time-consuming operations.

2. **Involve Operators Early**
   Let workers help train the cobot and provide feedback on safety and usability.

3. **Use Simulation and Digital Twins**
   Plan and optimize layouts before deployment using virtual models.

4. **Start with Hybrid Roles**
   Let cobots assist, not replace—gradually expanding autonomy.

5. **Monitor, Improve, Retrain**
   Use data from sensors and operator feedback to refine AI behavior over time.

Summary

AI-enabled collaborative robotics doesn't replace humans—it **enhances them**. By combining machine consistency with human adaptability, factories gain the best of both worlds: speed and judgment, precision and flexibility.

Cobots guided by AI open the door to **truly adaptive manufacturing**, where work flows not around robots—but through shared intelligence between people and machines.

In the next section, we'll explore how AI orchestrates the **autonomous movement of goods** within the factory through intelligent material handling and intralogistics.

6.5 Autonomous Material Handling and Smart Logistics

On any factory floor, material flow is the silent engine of productivity. It determines whether machines run smoothly, whether workers stay productive, and whether finished goods reach shipping on time. But traditional material handling—based on fixed routes, forklifts, and manual carts—is labor-intensive, prone to delays, and difficult to scale.

AI changes everything.

By powering autonomous mobile robots (AMRs), automated guided vehicles (AGVs), and intelligent warehouse orchestration, AI enables **smart, self-directed material flow**—making internal logistics faster, safer, and more efficient.

This isn't just automation. It's **self-navigation, self-optimization, and self-coordination.**

Traditional Material Handling: Limitations and Risks

Manual and semi-automated material transport systems face many issues:

- **Fixed-path AGVs** require magnetic strips, QR codes, or wires—making layout changes costly.

- **Forklifts** demand skilled operators and carry safety risks.

- **Human-driven carts** introduce variability and bottlenecks during shift changes or demand surges.

- **Disconnected systems** lead to overstock at workstations or idle machines waiting for inputs.

These inefficiencies result in:

- Increased lead times and WIP

- Safety incidents and near-misses

- Lower utilization of operators and machines

- Poor response to real-time production changes

The AI-Driven Alternative: Intelligent Intralogistics

AI powers autonomous material handling by combining:

- **Dynamic navigation algorithms**

- **Real-time sensor fusion and obstacle avoidance**

- **Task scheduling and fleet coordination**

- **Integration with MES, WMS, and ERP**

- **Continuous learning from environmental and traffic patterns**

Together, these capabilities turn transport units into **autonomous agents**—delivering materials where and when they're needed, without fixed paths or human intervention.

Core Components and Technologies

1. Autonomous Mobile Robots (AMRs)

- Navigate freely using LiDAR, SLAM (Simultaneous Localization and Mapping), and computer vision

- Detect people, objects, and unexpected obstacles

- Ideal for dynamic, multi-path environments like electronics, FMCG, or automotive assembly

2. AI Route Optimization and Traffic Control

- Algorithms dynamically reroute AMRs to avoid congestion

- Prioritize urgent tasks and balance workloads across fleets

- Predict dwell time at docks or stations to smooth handoffs

3. Task Scheduling and Demand Prediction

- AI systems forecast material needs based on WIP levels, job orders, and production rates

- Pre-position materials just in time—avoiding both starvation and clutter

4. Integrated Warehouse and Workstation Logistics

- AI coordinates storage, retrieval, and delivery in sync with production takt time

- Automates staging and decanting tasks using vision and robotic arms

Benefits of AI-Powered Material Handling

Benefit	Result
Faster Transport	Optimized routing reduces delivery delays
Lower Labor Costs	Fewer forklift operators or cart pushers needed
Higher Safety	AMRs detect people, avoid collisions
Greater Flexibility	Layouts can change without rewiring or reprogramming
Real-Time Responsiveness	Instantly adapt to order changes or line downtime
Increased Uptime	No shift handovers or breaks for AMRs

Case Study: Electronics Assembly Plant

Challenge:
Manual cart movement of trays between SMT lines and final assembly caused bottlenecks and uneven line balancing.

AI Solution:

- Deployed a fleet of 16 AMRs using LiDAR and SLAM navigation

- AI platform predicted part demand based on real-time job order data

- AMRs queued outside zones with visual alerts for handover

- **Results:**
- Delivery cycle time dropped by 47%

- Line downtime due to material wait reduced by 62%

- On-floor WIP inventory decreased by 21%

- Zero reported safety incidents in first year

Case Study: Food & Beverage Warehouse

Challenge:
Traditional AGVs couldn't handle changing aisle layouts or new SKUs without reprogramming, slowing throughput during promotional seasons.

AI Solution:

- Switched to vision-based AMRs with AI task scheduling

- Integrated AMR tasks with ERP-triggered pick lists

- AI traffic controller optimized flow during peak periods

Results:

- Warehouse throughput rose by 33%

- Changeover time for new layouts cut from 2 weeks to 3 days

- Labor hours reduced by 18% with improved worker satisfaction

Human-Robot Collaboration in Logistics

AI-enabled AMRs and cobots are designed to work **with** humans, not replace them.

- **Safe Zones and Predictive Stopping:** Robots slow down or stop near people

- **Visual Cues and Lights:** Help humans understand robot intentions

- **Voice or Gesture Commands:** Allow operators to summon or redirect robots

- **Load/Unload Interfaces:** Use AI vision to align with carts, pallets, or conveyors

These features ensure high safety, trust, and usability in mixed workspaces.

Deployment Guidelines

1. **Map Your Current Material Flow**
   Identify pain points, bottlenecks, and transport frequency hotspots.

2. **Start with High-Volume Routes**
   Choose areas with predictable flows and high labor cost for early ROI.

3. **Choose Scalable Platforms**
   Avoid fixed-path AGVs if flexibility is needed—favor AMRs with adaptive navigation.

4. **Integrate with Digital Systems**
   Connect to WMS, MES, or order management to automate task generation.

5. **Train and Involve Operators**
   Ensure human teams understand, trust, and collaborate with autonomous systems.

Summary

AI transforms material handling from a passive support function into a **strategic advantage**. By giving movement systems the ability to sense, decide, and adapt, manufacturers unlock faster cycle times, safer floors, and smarter factories.

When every delivery is precise, autonomous, and intelligent, the shop floor becomes a seamless, self-moving organism—always ready, always efficient.

In the next section, we'll explore how AI, digital twins, and real-time monitoring create a **virtual replica of the factory**—enabling predictive control, simulation, and decision support like never before.

6.6 Digital Twins and Real-Time Factory Intelligence

Imagine having a real-time replica of your factory—one that mirrors every process, machine, material, and variable on the floor. One that lets you test changes, simulate outcomes, predict bottlenecks, and make informed decisions before they impact operations.

This is the promise of **digital twins**—and with artificial intelligence, it becomes a dynamic, living system.

A digital twin isn't just a 3D model. It's a **connected, AI-powered mirror** of the physical factory—updating live with IoT sensor data, predicting system behavior, and enabling proactive optimization. It represents the convergence of data, simulation, and intelligence.

What Is a Digital Twin?

A **digital twin** is a virtual representation of a physical asset, process, or system that is continuously updated based on real-world data.

In manufacturing, this can include:

- Machines and equipment (health, usage, wear)

- Production processes (flow, yield, timing)

- Facility layouts and movement paths

- Inventory and materials

- Energy usage and environmental conditions

- Human-machine interactions

Digital twins operate in **real time**—providing visibility, analytics, and simulation capabilities for operators, planners, engineers, and executives alike.

The Role of AI in Digital Twins

AI transforms digital twins from static models into **intelligent systems** that learn and adapt:

- **Predictive analytics:** AI models forecast outcomes like cycle time, breakdowns, or scrap rates.

- **Process simulation:** Test "what-if" scenarios (e.g., new schedules, recipe changes, machine configurations).

- **Anomaly detection:** Spot deviations from normal behavior before issues escalate.

- **Optimization engines:** Recommend changes to maximize output or minimize cost.

- **Human-centric visualization:** AI filters data for relevance, guiding user attention.

With AI, digital twins evolve from descriptive tools into **prescriptive decision engines**.

Key Applications

1. Predictive Production Monitoring

- Monitor real-time KPIs (OEE, downtime, throughput, defect rate)

- Predict performance trends based on historical and live data

- Identify underperforming assets or operators and suggest interventions

Use Case:
An AI twin detects consistent micro-delays at a stamping station, predicts a shift in takt time, and recommends rescheduling downstream operations.

2. Maintenance and Reliability Forecasting

- Combine digital twin with sensor data to model wear and stress

- Predict time to failure for critical components

- Simulate impact of delayed repairs or part upgrades

Use Case:
A twin of a CNC machine simulates tool wear and suggests swap-out 36 hours before failure—saving costly downtime.

3. Production Simulation and Optimization

- Test alternative batch sizes, shift patterns, or product mixes

- Simulate new product introductions before they hit the line

- Adjust routing logic based on AI scenario modeling

Use Case:
Before launching a new part number, a twin runs 1,000 simulated production cycles to validate changeover times and material flow.

4. Factory Layout Planning and Bottleneck Analysis

- Visualize flow of materials, people, and machines

- Analyze space usage, congestion zones, and safety compliance

- Recommend layout changes to improve efficiency

Use Case:
An AI-driven layout twin identifies aisle congestion due to overlapping AMR and forklift routes—recommending rerouting paths for smoother logistics.

5. Energy and Sustainability Optimization

- Monitor energy consumption across zones, lines, or machines

- Model carbon impact of different schedules or suppliers

- Optimize power usage during peak hours using predictive AI

Use Case:
The digital twin of a furnace line schedules high-load jobs during off-peak hours, cutting energy costs by 19% weekly.

Components of a Digital Twin Platform

- **IoT Sensors:** Feed real-time data (temperature, vibration, speed, etc.)

- **MES/ERP Integration:** Connect business logic and orders to operations

- **3D Visualization or Process Maps:** Show spatial or flow-based relationships

- **AI Models:** Analyze, predict, and prescribe actions

- **Simulation Engine:** Test changes before applying them

- **User Interface and Dashboards:** Enable human interaction and control

Case Study: Aerospace Parts Factory

Challenge:
Complex scheduling, long changeover times, and quality defects in turbine blade production.

Solution:

- Built a digital twin that modeled every asset, job, operator, and movement

- AI predicted delays based on operator load, machine temperature, and queue length

- Ran hourly simulations to optimize batch order and resource allocation

Results:

- OEE improved by 14%

- Scrap rate dropped by 22%

- Average job completion time cut by 3.6 hours

Deployment Guidelines

1. **Start with a Focused Scope**
   Begin with one line, machine group, or process that impacts key KPIs.

2. **Map Data Sources**
   Ensure clean, reliable feeds from PLCs, MES, SCADA, and sensors.

3. **Build and Validate the Twin**
   Use historical and live data to calibrate model behavior. Validate predictions.

4. **Layer in AI Gradually**
   Begin with alerts and dashboards, then expand into simulations and prescriptive logic.

5. **Train Users**
   Empower teams to interpret, trust, and act on digital twin insights.

6. **Scale Across the Network**
   Once proven, deploy sitewide or across facilities for network-level visibility.

Summary

A digital twin with embedded AI is more than a mirror—it's a **strategic advisor, performance coach, and simulation lab** rolled into one. It enables factories to anticipate problems, test changes safely, and continuously improve—all without disrupting the floor.

As complexity rises and agility becomes essential, the AI-powered digital twin is the key to unlocking **self-aware, self-optimizing factories** of the future.

In the final section of this chapter, we'll consolidate all these technologies into an overarching view of the **intelligent factory**, offering a roadmap for transformation.

Conclusion: The Intelligent Factory in Action

The factory floor has always been the beating heart of manufacturing. But today, it is evolving—from a place of mechanical repetition to one of **cognitive coordination**. From reactive control to proactive intelligence. From hardwired automation to **learning systems that sense, think, and adapt in real time**.

This chapter has shown that AI is not a singular tool—it is an ecosystem of capabilities that, when combined, transform the entire production environment.

What We've Covered

We explored six critical domains of AI-driven factory transformation:

1. **Predictive Maintenance:**
   AI-powered systems anticipate failures before they occur, reducing downtime and extending machine life.

2. **Real-Time Process Optimization:**
   Machine learning models adjust process variables on the fly to boost yield, quality, and energy efficiency.

3. **Computer Vision and Inspection:**
   Deep learning enables smarter defect detection, quality verification, and robot guidance—outpacing manual and rule-based inspection.

4. **Collaborative Robotics (Cobots):**
   AI enhances robot safety, perception, and learning—enabling seamless human-machine collaboration across flexible tasks.

5. **Autonomous Material Handling:**
   AMRs and intelligent logistics platforms move goods efficiently with real-time

navigation, task scheduling, and obstacle avoidance.

6. **Digital Twins:**
   Virtual replicas powered by AI simulate, predict, and optimize operations continuously—making the invisible visible and the complex controllable.

Each of these pillars stands strong alone—but together, they form the foundation of the **intelligent factory**.

The Integrated Vision: AI as the Factory Nervous System

In the intelligent factory:

- Machines don't just run—they **communicate** their health and performance.

- Robots don't just repeat—they **learn** and adapt based on interaction.

- Processes don't just follow rules—they **optimize themselves** in real time.

- Material doesn't just move—it **flows autonomously**, guided by AI logistics.

- Operators don't just monitor—they **collaborate with AI**, making decisions augmented by real-time insights.

- Leaders don't just review reports—they **simulate, plan, and act** using digital twins.

AI becomes the **nervous system** of the modern factory—sensing everything, interpreting patterns, and orchestrating intelligent action.

Roadmap to Implementation

To build an intelligent factory, manufacturers can
follow a practical progression:

1. **Digitize and Connect First**
    Ensure sensors, PLCs, MES, and ERP
    systems are integrated and producing
    usable data.

2. **Start with Targeted Pilots**
    Apply AI to one use case with high
    ROI—such as predictive maintenance or
    defect detection.

3. **Build Cross-Functional Teams**
    Combine data scientists, engineers,
    operators, and IT to bridge the gap
    between AI design and factory execution.

4. **Create Feedback Loops**
    Allow systems to learn from operator
    feedback, quality outcomes, and
    long-term performance data.

5. **Scale Modularly**
    Expand to more lines, sites, or use
    cases once results are validated.

6. **Embrace a Culture of Learning**
   Train workers not just to use AI—but to
   improve it, monitor it, and innovate with it.

The Human-AI Partnership

At its core, the intelligent factory is not just about automation—it's about **augmentation**. AI elevates human capabilities, reduces routine strain, and unlocks higher-value contributions from workers and managers alike.

The most successful factories will be those where people and AI work **together**—not in competition, but in collaboration.

Looking Ahead

As we close this chapter, we shift our focus from the factory inward—to the **enterprise itself**. In the next chapter, we'll explore how AI empowers **strategic decision-making, product design, and end-to-end business integration**—turning data into direction and insight into impact.

Because the intelligent factory is just one part of the **AI-powered enterprise**—and the future of manufacturing is being written not only on the shop floor, but in the boardroom.

7.0 Introduction: From Data to Direction

In today's fast-moving world, data is everywhere. From factory sensors and customer feedback to supply chain signals and financial metrics, manufacturers generate a torrent of information every second. But data alone isn't enough.

What truly matters is **what you do with it**.

Artificial intelligence offers the enterprise a new kind of leadership tool—not just for operations, but for **strategic thinking, design innovation, and enterprise-wide coordination**. AI transforms data into direction, enabling companies to act with clarity, confidence, and speed.

This chapter explores how AI moves upstream—into the executive suite, the R&D lab, the finance office, and the product roadmap—to create an **intelligent enterprise**.

Why Enterprise Decision-Making Needs AI

Traditional decision-making often suffers from:

- **Information overload** — too much data, not enough time

- **Siloed systems** — different teams with disconnected insights

- **Lagging reports** — decisions based on what happened weeks ago

- **Gut-driven strategy** — intuition outweighing evidence

- **Lack of agility** — plans that can't adapt to change

As complexity increases, so does the cost of indecision or misdirection.

AI addresses these challenges by acting as a **real-time advisor, scenario planner, and signal amplifier**. It connects the dots across systems, spots patterns humans can't, and recommends actions that align with corporate goals.

AI's Role Across Enterprise Functions

Function	How AI Adds Strategic Value
Executive Leadership	Simulates strategic scenarios, forecasts risk, measures impact
Finance	Automates forecasting, detects anomalies, optimizes capital
Marketing & Sales	Analyzes buyer behavior, predicts churn, customizes campaigns
Product Development	Identifies trends, accelerates design iteration, predicts success
HR & Workforce	Forecasts attrition, suggests skill development, improves hiring
Sustainability & ESG	Tracks emissions, benchmarks performance, recommends improvements

AI transforms isolated functions into **collaborative, data-driven decision ecosystems**.

The New Decision Engine: AI + Human Judgment

AI doesn't replace leadership—it enhances it. The best outcomes come when human vision and machine intelligence work together:

- **Humans set the goals**

- **AI analyzes the paths**

- **Humans apply context**

- **AI monitors the signals**

- **Together, they adapt**

This partnership ensures that decisions are **strategic, scalable, and grounded in real-time insight**.

Chapter Preview

In the sections ahead, we'll explore how AI
enables:

- Executive dashboards that simulate
  strategic shifts in real time

- Financial models that self-update and
  detect anomalies

- Product R&D platforms that learn from
  user feedback

- ESG reporting tools that analyze
  sustainability performance

- Cross-functional decision hubs powered
  by AI integration

With case studies, frameworks, and practical
deployment advice, this chapter shows how
manufacturers can go beyond digital
transformation—and build the **intelligent
enterprise** of the future.

7.1 AI for Strategic Planning and Executive Simulation

Strategic planning has long relied on periodic reviews, static forecasts, and executive intuition. But in a world where markets shift overnight, customers evolve constantly, and supply chains face daily disruption, this approach is no longer enough.

To lead in today's environment, executives need **decision velocity**—the ability to simulate, assess, and act on scenarios with both speed and precision. Artificial intelligence delivers that velocity by enabling leaders to visualize outcomes, test assumptions, and navigate complexity through real-time simulation.

This is the era of **executive intelligence augmented by AI**—where strategy is no longer static, but continuously informed by live, predictive data.

The Limits of Traditional Strategic Planning

Most traditional planning processes suffer from:

- **Quarterly or annual cadence** that fails to adapt to sudden changes

- **Spreadsheet-based models** with rigid assumptions

- **Siloed departmental input** that misses cross-functional impact

- **Backward-looking analytics** rather than forward-looking simulations

- **Overreliance on static KPIs** without understanding dynamic cause-effect links

AI addresses these weaknesses by modeling the enterprise as a **living, responsive system**—capable of evaluating countless scenarios and guiding real-time adaptation.

What AI Brings to Strategic Planning

Capability	Description
Scenario Simulation	Test "what-if" strategies across markets, supply chains, and operations
Dynamic Forecasting	Continuously update revenue, cost, or demand projections based on live data
Risk Prediction	Detect potential disruptions or underperformance before KPIs show trouble
Resource Optimization	Recommend shifts in budget, headcount, or investment based on modeled outcomes
Causal Analysis	Identify key drivers of performance (e.g., which factors truly impact margin growth)

Decision Guidance	Provide ranked action paths aligned with goals, constraints, and timelines

AI becomes a **strategic co-pilot**, not just a reporting engine.

Executive Dashboards with Embedded AI

Next-generation dashboards do more than show KPIs. They explain **why trends are happening**, predict **what's likely next**, and recommend **how to respond**.

Features include:

- Natural language summaries ("Revenue is trending +4% above forecast due to rising orders in Region B")

- Anomaly alerts with root cause hypotheses

- Scenario toggles (e.g., "What happens to EBIT if raw materials rise 8%?")

- Forecast comparisons across departments and time horizons

- Strategic alignment scoring (how close each plan gets to target goals)

These tools turn every executive review into a **simulation session**—grounded in data, focused on action.

Real-Time Strategic Simulation: Key Use Cases

1. Market Entry Planning

AI models simulate revenue, costs, and competitive responses for entering new regions. Scenarios can factor in:

- Local customer demand

- Regulatory or tax impacts

- Logistics and supplier readiness

- Political or currency risk

- Talent availability

2. Capacity Expansion

Test outcomes of opening new production lines, shifting volumes between plants, or outsourcing.

3. Price and Margin Strategy

Evaluate the impact of changing price points on volume, profit, and competitor positioning using demand elasticity models.

4. M&A Impact Simulation

Model post-merger synergies, overlap risks, and

culture integration scenarios using HR, finance, and operations data.

Case Study: Global Industrial Manufacturer

Challenge:
The leadership team struggled to align regional business units on a global growth plan. Assumptions varied, and traditional planning took months.

AI Solution:

- Deployed an AI strategy engine that pulled data from finance, sales, production, and HR systems

- Modeled revenue, margin, and resource utilization across 15 potential investment paths

- Visualized scenarios as impact charts and risk surfaces

Results:

- Strategic alignment across regions achieved in 5 weeks (vs. 4 months)

- $88M in forecasted cost avoidance through optimized capital allocation

- 3 new initiatives greenlit with scenario-backed confidence

Implementation Blueprint

1. **Start with a Strategic Pain Point**
   Is the issue growth uncertainty, cost pressure, expansion timing, or resource prioritization?

2. **Gather Cross-Functional Data**
   Pull inputs from sales, operations, HR, finance, and supply chain to fuel models.

3. **Deploy a Strategic Simulation Tool**
   Use platforms that support real-time modeling, visualization, and AI-assisted forecasting.

4. **Train Executive Teams**
   Equip leaders to explore "what-if" scenarios, not just review dashboards.

5. **Integrate AI Into Planning Cycles**
   Move from quarterly to continuous planning—where AI informs decisions weekly or even daily.

Key Success Factors

- **Model Transparency:** Ensure executives can understand how AI arrived at recommendations.

- **Scenario Framing:** Start with strategic questions, not just data dumps.

- **Cross-Silo Buy-In:** Involve all stakeholders early so assumptions are aligned.

- **Iteration Over Perfection:** Let AI guide dynamic planning, not enforce rigid predictions.

- **Governance and Ethics:** Review AI-recommended strategies for fairness, compliance, and unintended consequences.

Summary

AI empowers leaders to stop guessing and start simulating. By turning plans into models and strategies into adaptive scenarios, AI helps executives make **faster, more confident, and more resilient decisions**—even in times of uncertainty.

Strategic planning becomes a live process—not a document on a shelf.

In the next section, we'll explore how AI transforms **enterprise finance**—from forecasting and reporting to fraud detection and investment modeling.

7.2 AI in Financial Planning and Decision Support

Finance is the backbone of strategic decision-making. It links every function in the enterprise through budgets, forecasts, investments, and risk. Yet too often, finance operates in hindsight—focused on closing books, generating static reports, and explaining what already happened.

Artificial intelligence turns this model on its head.

AI empowers finance teams to **forecast dynamically, allocate capital intelligently, and detect risks proactively**—transforming finance into a forward-looking command center that supports real-time business navigation.

The Limitations of Traditional Finance Models

Despite their central role, finance departments often struggle with:

- **Manual budgeting processes** and error-prone spreadsheets

- **Lagging reports** that reflect outdated data

- **One-size-fits-all forecasts** that don't adapt to volatility

- **Limited capacity for scenario testing or root cause analysis**

- **Siloed data sources** that don't connect sales, ops, and finance

These challenges slow down decision-making and limit finance's ability to guide strategy.

How AI Transforms Financial Planning

Capability	AI-Enabled Advantage
Dynamic Forecasting	Models adapt in real time to changes in sales, costs, or markets
Anomaly Detection	Flags unusual transactions, expenses, or KPI shifts instantly
Predictive Cash Flow	Projects future inflows and outflows based on patterns and signals
Budget Optimization	Allocates spending based on ROI models and priority ranking
Investment Modeling	Simulates outcomes of capital projects, M&A, or expansions
Narrative Generation	Automatically creates human-readable financial summaries

AI empowers finance teams to shift from reporting to **recommendation**, from control to **collaboration**, and from defense to **offense**.

Real-Time Financial Forecasting

With AI, forecasts become:

- **Granular:** Updated by SKU, region, or channel

- **Rolling:** Continuously refined, not just once per quarter

- **Context-aware:** Informed by operations, sales, supply chain, and macro data

- **Actionable:** Tied directly to business decisions like hiring, pricing, or expansion

Example:
Instead of quarterly revenue forecasts, an AI model can predict daily trends by analyzing sales, website traffic, market signals, and promotions—adjusting forecasts on the fly.

AI-Driven Budgeting and Resource Allocation

AI helps CFOs and controllers:

- **Prioritize spend** based on historical ROI, alignment with goals, or seasonal demand

- **Simulate tradeoffs** between funding options

- **Prevent budget padding** or underestimation through predictive variance detection

AI also enables **driver-based planning**, where financial outcomes are linked to operational levers (e.g., "If machine uptime improves by 5%, margin grows by 1.2%").

Anomaly Detection and Financial Risk Prevention

AI models can learn normal transaction and performance patterns, then flag deviations:

- Fraudulent transactions or duplicate payments

- Unusual expense spikes or declining margins

- Unauthorized vendor additions or invoice mismatches

- KPI anomalies (e.g., unexplained drop in gross margin in a region)

This makes audits faster, risk management more proactive, and compliance stronger.

Capital Investment and Project Modeling

AI supports scenario planning for major financial decisions:

- Expansion projects

- Automation investments

- Mergers and acquisitions

- Product development initiatives

By modeling historical project data, market signals, and risk variables, AI can:

- Score investment alternatives

- Simulate payback timelines and IRR ranges

- Recommend optimal capital allocation across projects

This makes investment committees smarter and faster—and improves return on capital.

Case Study: Global Manufacturing Conglomerate

Challenge:
Monthly forecasts took 12+ days, required data from 9 systems, and failed to detect early profit erosion.

AI Solution:

- Deployed an AI forecasting engine integrated with sales, procurement, and operations

- Used anomaly detection to flag expense spikes and margin dips

- Simulated impact of pricing and cost changes on EBITDA in real time

Results:

- Forecasting time reduced from 12 days to under 36 hours

- $21M in early risk avoidance across four regions

- Executive dashboard adoption rose by 240%

Implementation Roadmap

1. **Start with a Forecasting Pilot**
   Choose one region, business unit, or P&L line to test AI forecasting.

2. **Centralize and Clean Data**
   Integrate finance, sales, supply chain, and HR data into a unified model.

3. **Use Explainable AI (XAI)**
   Ensure finance teams understand why predictions or alerts are made.

4. **Connect to Decision Processes**
   Link AI insights to capital planning, hiring, pricing, or investment decisions.

5. **Scale with Governance**
   Establish controls, audits, and oversight as AI becomes part of core financial operations.

Skills and Culture Shift

For finance professionals, AI adoption requires:

- **Upskilling in analytics, modeling, and AI literacy**

- **Shifting from data gathering to data questioning**

- **Collaborating with IT, operations, and business units**

- **Balancing AI automation with judgment, ethics, and context**

The CFO of the future is a **data strategist and AI translator**—not just a financial controller.

Summary

AI transforms finance from a back-office ledger to a front-line driver of strategic agility. By forecasting dynamically, allocating wisely, and flagging risk early, AI empowers financial leaders to act with speed, foresight, and confidence.

In the next section, we'll explore how AI supports **product innovation and customer-centered design**—helping enterprises bring better offerings to market, faster than ever before.

7.3 AI in Product Design and Innovation Strategy

Innovation is the lifeblood of competitive advantage. Yet in many enterprises, product development remains slow, expensive, and guesswork-driven. Teams rely on historical sales, intuition, and limited user testing to design tomorrow's products—often missing what the market actually wants.

Artificial intelligence changes the game.

AI enables enterprises to **analyze trends, generate designs, simulate performance, and predict customer adoption**—all before a single prototype is built. It turns innovation into a data-driven discipline, where creativity is amplified by computation and success is forecasted before launch.

Challenges in Traditional Product Development

Product teams face mounting pressure to deliver:

- Faster time-to-market

- Higher personalization

- Better sustainability

- Stronger differentiation

- Lower cost and risk

Yet traditional methods struggle with:

- **Slow feedback loops** from prototypes to real-world performance

- **Limited customer input** due to costly surveys or small focus groups

- **Siloed design, marketing, and engineering functions**

- **Inability to simulate design-market fit early in the process**

AI addresses these issues with tools that **see ahead, simulate outcomes, and shape strategy**.

How AI Enhances Product Design and Innovation

Function	AI Capabilities
Trend Analysis	NLP and data mining to detect emerging needs across markets
Idea Generation	Generative AI proposes design options, configurations, or concepts
Customer Insight	AI analyzes reviews, support tickets, and social media to surface pain points
Design Simulation	Predicts performance, manufacturability, and material stress
Market Forecasting	Predicts demand and adoption rates using historical and external signals
Portfolio Optimization	Recommends which products to accelerate, delay, or sunset

AI turns the product innovation process into an **iterative, insight-rich engine**—aligned with real user needs and market conditions.

Real-World Use Cases

1. AI-Assisted Concept Design
Tools like generative design platforms use AI to create thousands of design alternatives based on constraints (e.g., weight, material, cost). Engineers select the best options—cutting cycle times dramatically.

2. Voice of Customer (VoC) Mining
AI scans online reviews, call center transcripts, and forum discussions to extract unmet needs, recurring complaints, and desired features.

3. Demand Forecasting for New Products
Machine learning predicts likely adoption rates for new SKUs or features—based on product similarity, channel readiness, price sensitivity, and competitor activity.

4. Digital Twin for Product Testing
Simulates product use conditions (heat, stress, moisture, human interaction) before physical prototypes are created—saving cost and speeding design validation.

5. AI-Driven Portfolio Management
Analyzes performance, margins, and cannibalization risks across a full product line—guiding investment toward winners and phasing out laggards.

Case Study: Consumer Electronics Firm

Challenge:
Product cycles were slowing due to repeated prototype rework and late discovery of customer dissatisfaction.

AI Solution:

- Used NLP to analyze 1.2 million user reviews and 200K service records

- Identified top 5 pain points by product category

- Used generative design to create housing options addressing grip, durability, and aesthetic concerns

- Forecasted likely demand curves by price point and market

Results:

- Concept-to-prototype cycle cut by 40%

- Customer satisfaction in pilot market rose 23%

- New product launch forecasted 12% higher margin than previous models

Implementation Best Practices

1. **Begin with Data-Rich Areas**
   Start in product lines where reviews, usage data, or warranty claims are abundant.

2. **Combine AI with Human-Centered Design**
   Let designers interpret AI insights through the lens of empathy and creativity.

3. **Use Modular Platforms**
   Deploy AI in discrete steps—trend analysis, then concept scoring, then simulation—before scaling.

4. **Integrate Across Functions**
   Link R&D, marketing, customer support, and sales so all innovation is guided by shared intelligence.

5. **Involve Product Managers and Engineers Early**
   Ensure they trust AI outputs and see them as decision accelerators—not replacements.

Risks and Ethical Considerations

- **Over-Optimization for Short-Term Trends:** Balance data-driven insights with long-term brand vision.

- **Privacy and Consent in User Data:** Ensure VoC data use complies with data protection laws.

- **Bias in AI Training Data:** Monitor for exclusion or skew that may miss key user groups.

- **Loss of Intuition:** Preserve human creativity and passion in final decision-making.

Summary

AI doesn't replace innovation—it **amplifies it**. By making sense of complexity, predicting demand, and accelerating ideation, AI helps enterprises bring better products to market, faster—and with more confidence in their success.

In the next section, we'll explore how AI enhances **sustainability and ESG strategy**—empowering enterprises to reduce emissions, increase transparency, and meet global regulatory expectations through data and automation.

7.4 AI for Sustainability, ESG, and Responsible Manufacturing

In the modern manufacturing landscape, sustainability is no longer a choice—it's a competitive imperative. Investors demand transparency. Regulators require compliance. Customers reward responsible brands. And internal stakeholders seek purpose-driven work.

Artificial intelligence helps manufacturers transform environmental, social, and governance (ESG) goals from abstract aspirations into **data-driven, measurable, and actionable outcomes**.

Whether it's reducing carbon footprints, managing ethical sourcing, or ensuring workplace safety, AI provides the visibility, analytics, and automation to make sustainable operations not just possible—but profitable.

Challenges in ESG Execution

Despite growing commitments to ESG, enterprises face several hurdles:

- **Data fragmentation:** Sustainability data is scattered across sites, systems, and suppliers

- **Manual reporting burdens:** ESG audits are time-consuming and error-prone

- **Limited traceability:** Tracking emissions or labor practices across tiers of the supply chain is difficult

- **Inconsistent benchmarks:** No universal framework exists for ESG scoring

- **Reactive compliance:** Actions are often in response to regulation, not guided by prediction or strategy

AI solves these issues by enabling **proactive, automated, and transparent ESG management** at scale.

Key Applications of AI in ESG and Sustainability

Focus Area	AI-Enabled Capabilities
Carbon Tracking	Estimate scope 1, 2, and 3 emissions using AI models and IoT data
Energy Optimization	Predict energy demand and shift usage to reduce cost and emissions
Waste Minimization	Identify root causes of material loss, scrap, or overproduction
Sustainable Sourcing	Monitor supplier ESG scores and detect violations via NLP/news analysis
Workforce Safety	Use vision AI to detect PPE compliance, unsafe behavior, or fatigue
Regulatory Reporting	Auto-generate disclosures aligned to GRI, SASB, or CSRD frameworks

AI makes sustainability **real-time, predictive, and verifiable**—enabling organizations to move from reactive reporting to continuous improvement.

Real-World Use Cases

1. Energy-Aware Scheduling
AI forecasts energy demand based on production plans and market rates, then adjusts operations to avoid peak usage periods—saving money and reducing CO_2.

2. Predictive Carbon Footprint
Digital twins combined with AI simulate the total carbon output of a product—from sourcing to delivery—before it's even made, enabling design-stage improvements.

3. AI-Powered Supply Chain Auditing
NLP engines analyze supplier documents, media, and court records to detect ESG risks like child labor, deforestation, or pollution—even in Tier 2 and Tier 3 vendors.

4. Smart Waste Monitoring
AI vision systems identify sources of scrap or defective materials in real time, helping teams intervene earlier and reduce landfill contributions.

5. Automated ESG Reporting
AI extracts relevant data from production systems, matches it to standards like CDP or TCFD, and generates audit-ready

disclosures—freeing ESG teams from manual compilation.

Case Study: Global Packaging Manufacturer

Challenge:
The company committed to net-zero by 2040 but struggled to track energy use and carbon across 28 plants globally.

AI Solution:

- Deployed AI models that learned from utility bills, sensor feeds, and production data

- Modeled Scope 1 & 2 emissions by machine, shift, and region

- Suggested process improvements (e.g., batch heating, off-peak operation) to lower impact

Results:

- Achieved 11.3% emissions reduction in year one

- Generated real-time ESG dashboards for plant managers

- Passed independent audit with full AI
  data lineage

Implementation Guidelines

1. **Set Measurable Goals First**
   Define KPIs like GHG reduction, energy intensity, safety incidents, or supplier ESG scores.

2. **Instrument the Right Data**
   Collect data from machines, sensors, buildings, transportation systems, and supplier portals.

3. **Build an AI ESG Platform**
   Use AI tools with pre-trained models for sustainability metrics, scenario analysis, and compliance tracking.

4. **Integrate With Reporting Frameworks**
   Map AI outputs to required disclosures: GRI, SASB, CSRD, SEC climate rules, etc.

5. **Enable Frontline Ownership**
   Provide operators, procurement teams, and logistics managers with dashboards showing their real-time sustainability impact.

AI for Social and Governance Dimensions

While environmental metrics dominate ESG, AI also supports:

- **Diversity and Inclusion Auditing:** NLP scans HR documents to detect gendered language or bias

- **Ethical Hiring Patterns:** Machine learning assesses candidate pipelines for demographic equity

- **Workplace Safety Analytics:** Predicts incidents based on machine usage, shift patterns, or environmental conditions

- **Governance Risk Detection:** AI flags inconsistencies in board reports, internal controls, or third-party relationships

By enhancing transparency, AI builds trust with investors, regulators, and society.

Ethical Considerations

As AI is used to ensure ethics, it must also be used **ethically**:

- Maintain privacy when analyzing HR or social data

- Avoid embedding bias into ESG models

- Ensure traceability of AI recommendations in audits

- Validate AI outputs with domain experts and regulatory advisors

Summary

AI empowers enterprises to turn sustainability promises into performance. By measuring impact in real time, simulating future outcomes, and guiding corrective action, AI becomes the engine of responsible growth.

In the next and final section of this chapter, we'll explore how to **integrate all enterprise AI functions**—from supply chain and finance to product and ESG—into a cohesive, intelligent business system.

7.5 Integrated AI Strategy Across the Enterprise

The power of artificial intelligence is not fully realized when it's confined to silos—used in isolation by operations, finance, or R&D. The real transformation begins when AI systems are **connected, collaborative, and enterprise-wide**.

An integrated AI strategy turns every function into a **node of intelligence**, all feeding into a shared network that sees more, learns faster, and acts with unity. This is the foundation of the truly intelligent enterprise—one that doesn't just work harder, but **thinks smarter** across every level of the organization.

The Problem with Siloed AI

While many companies are piloting AI across different departments, common issues include:

- **Duplicated efforts** across teams using separate AI vendors and tools

- **Conflicting models** generating inconsistent forecasts or decisions

- **Data fragmentation**, where key insights remain locked in departmental systems

- **Missed synergies** between interdependent functions (e.g., product, finance, and supply chain)

- **Governance and compliance challenges** without centralized oversight

The result is a patchwork of disconnected smart systems—smart in parts, but not **strategically intelligent** as a whole.

The Vision: A Unified AI Operating System

An integrated enterprise AI strategy enables:

Element	Enterprise-Wide Outcome
Connected Data Lakes	One source of truth across departments and functions
Cross-Domain Models	AI that understands how sales, operations, finance, and ESG impact each other
Real-Time Decision Loops	Continuous, live decision-making across the business
Governance Layer	Security, ethics, and compliance baked into every model and interaction
Feedback Integration	Learnings from one function improve others (e.g., product feedback refines forecasting)

This approach creates a **neural network of enterprise intelligence**—learning and adapting at the organizational level.

Strategic Foundations of Integration

1. AI as a Shared Capability, Not a Department
AI should be embedded across teams—but governed centrally to ensure consistency, reuse, and efficiency.

2. Cloud-Based Architecture
Use centralized platforms (e.g., Azure, AWS, GCP) to host models, data, and APIs that serve all departments in real time.

3. Model Reusability
Avoid duplication by creating shared AI models (e.g., demand forecasting, customer churn, cost optimization) that can be adapted across functions.

4. Unified Data Governance
Implement enterprise-wide data standards, tagging, and access protocols.

5. Cross-Functional AI Hubs
Create a Center of Excellence (CoE) that supports distributed innovation while maintaining strategic alignment.

How Integration Looks in Practice

Product Design feeds Finance:
Forecasted demand from AI market models adjusts investment allocations and inventory planning.

Finance supports Supply Chain:
AI budget constraints inform vendor selection and procurement priorities.

ESG aligns with Operations:
Sustainability targets integrated into production planning via emissions-aware scheduling models.

Customer Feedback loops to R&D:
AI-summarized sentiment analysis feeds directly into product improvement roadmaps.

Executive Dashboards unify all:
A real-time cockpit shows top KPIs and risk indicators across functions—powered by live AI predictions.

Case Study: Global Advanced Manufacturing Enterprise

Challenge:
Departments used different AI vendors and tools—leading to data inconsistencies, delayed decisions, and compliance risks.

Solution:

- Established an AI Integration Office reporting to both CIO and COO

- Standardized data pipelines and created an internal AI app marketplace

- Connected use cases across finance, product, operations, and ESG

- Built an enterprise dashboard for executives with live AI inputs across functions

Results:

- Reduced AI development costs by 37%

- Time-to-decision accelerated by 60%

- Cross-functional initiatives increased by 4X in 12 months

- Identified $190M in value from AI synergies across teams

Implementation Roadmap

1. **Audit Current AI Usage**
   Inventory all AI tools, models, vendors, and data platforms in use today.

2. **Define the AI Operating Model**
   Determine which capabilities will be centralized, federated, or distributed.

3. **Invest in Scalable Infrastructure**
   Adopt cloud-native platforms, data lakes, and ML ops tools that support multi-function usage.

4. **Create Enterprise-Wide Use Case Templates**
   Design modular AI apps (e.g., pricing optimizer, lead scorer, risk detector) reusable across domains.

5. **Build a Culture of Collaboration**
   Train teams on AI literacy, ethics, and shared innovation incentives.

Risks and Mitigations

Risk	Mitigation Strategy
Model Overlap or Conflict	Enforce a registry of models and domains
Data Privacy Concerns	Apply role-based access and data masking across pipelines
Shadow AI Development	Create incentives for teams to share models and code
Governance Lags	Embed compliance and ethical checks into model lifecycle

Summary

Integrated AI is the capstone of digital transformation. It connects the insights of every function, the power of every model, and the vision of every leader—into a unified intelligence engine for the entire enterprise.

This is how companies go beyond isolated wins and build sustained, system-wide advantage.

With Chapter 7 complete, we now prepare to move toward the **final chapters of the book**, where we examine the roadmap to scale, the future of AI in manufacturing, and how to lead the transformation.

8.0 Introduction: From Experiments to Enterprise AI

Across the manufacturing world, AI pilot programs are showing promise—reducing downtime, improving forecasts, optimizing energy, and enhancing quality. But while the wins are real, many organizations struggle to move beyond isolated use cases. Too often, AI remains a **lab experiment**, not a core part of how the business runs.

The challenge now is to **scale**.

Scaling AI means creating the systems, talent, governance, and culture that allow dozens—or even hundreds—of AI applications to thrive. It means making AI **repeatable, reliable, and responsible** at every level of the enterprise.

This chapter focuses on how to go from **proof-of-concept to platform**—turning innovation into transformation.

The Scaling Gap

Research shows that while over 80% of manufacturers have launched AI pilots, fewer than 20% have operationalized them at scale. Common challenges include:

- **Lack of leadership ownership**

- **Data silos and inconsistent infrastructure**

- **Shortage of AI-literate talent**

- **No model lifecycle management**

- **Unclear ROI and value tracking**

- **Ethical and regulatory uncertainty**

Without deliberate strategy, AI becomes fragmented and fragile—leading to disappointment rather than disruption.

What Scaling Requires

To succeed, scaling AI must be treated as **an enterprise change program**, not just a technology initiative. It requires investment across three pillars:

Pillar	Focus Area
Governance	Trust, ethics, compliance, model approval, risk management
Talent and Culture	Skills development, cross-functional collaboration, AI fluency
Architecture	Scalable infrastructure, data pipelines, model operations, reusability

When aligned, these pillars ensure that AI can grow—safely, strategically, and sustainably.

Chapter Overview

In the sections that follow, we'll explore:

- **Governance frameworks** to ensure AI is explainable, compliant, and auditable

- **Talent strategies** to build internal expertise and attract top AI professionals

- **AI literacy programs** to empower all employees—not just data scientists

- **Enterprise architectures** that support modular, multi-use-case scaling

- **ModelOps and lifecycle management** for continuous improvement and monitoring

- **Scaling success metrics** to track adoption, value creation, and trust

The goal: to help manufacturing leaders **turn AI from innovation islands into a connected, enterprise-wide engine of growth**.

The Stakes Are High

Scaling AI isn't just about staying competitive.
It's about survival in a world of constant volatility,
tighter regulations, talent shortages, and rising
customer expectations.

Those who succeed will:

- Innovate faster

- Operate leaner

- Adapt sooner

- Serve smarter

- Grow sustainably

Those who don't may find themselves locked in
pilot purgatory—outpaced by more agile,
intelligent competitors.

Summary

Scaling AI is not a technical problem—it's a
leadership priority. It requires executive

commitment, clear governance, strong architecture, and a deep investment in people. This chapter is your roadmap for building all of it—so your AI ambitions don't stall, but soar.

8.1 AI Governance: Trust, Transparency, and Control at Scale

As artificial intelligence spreads across the enterprise—from forecasting and quality control to hiring, pricing, and ESG—so too does the responsibility to ensure it operates safely, ethically, and under control. Governance is no longer optional. It is the foundation for scaling AI with **confidence and accountability**.

AI governance ensures that systems are **auditable, explainable, fair, secure, and aligned** with both regulatory standards and corporate values. It builds **trust with employees, customers, and regulators**, turning risk into resilience and chaos into clarity.

Why AI Governance Matters Now

Without governance, scaled AI can lead to:

- **Regulatory violations** (e.g., GDPR, CSRD, OSHA, SEC disclosure rules)

- **Reputational damage** from biased or unethical decisions

- **Model drift** that silently degrades performance over time

- **Black-box algorithms** that cannot be explained in audits or litigation

- **Lack of accountability** for outcomes when humans defer blindly to AI

As AI shifts from back-office pilots to front-line automation and executive decision support, **strong governance becomes the guardrail** that keeps innovation on track.

Key Principles of AI Governance

Principle	Description
Transparency	Ability to explain how and why a model made a decision
Fairness	Avoiding bias and ensuring equitable outcomes across users
Accountability	Clearly defined ownership for each model's design, deployment, and outcome
Security & Privacy	Safeguarding model inputs, outputs, and training data
Compliance	Alignment with internal policy and external regulations
Traceability	Full lifecycle logging of model versions, inputs, feedback, and updates

What AI Governance Covers

AI governance spans the full model lifecycle:

1. **Model Design & Development**

   - Ethical design reviews

   - Bias detection and mitigation

   - Data quality and representativeness

2. **Model Validation**

   - Testing across multiple datasets and scenarios

   - Accuracy and robustness benchmarks

   - Explainability scoring and documentation

3. **Deployment & Monitoring**

   - Role-based access control

   - Performance drift detection

- Alert thresholds for accuracy, bias, or outliers

4. **Review & Retraining**

   - Scheduled model audits

   - Human-in-the-loop oversight

   - Feedback loop integration

5. **Incident Management**

   - Protocols for error or harm detection

   - Transparent communication and remediation pathways

Enterprise Governance Models

Model Type	Characteristics
Centralized AI Council	One cross-functional body sets standards and reviews models
Federated Governance	Individual units apply standards with oversight from a core group
Hybrid Model	Core team builds frameworks; business units execute and escalate exceptions

Best-in-class companies appoint **Chief AI Ethics Officers** or embed AI governance in Risk, Compliance, or Data Office functions.

Case Study: Industrial AI Governance Framework

Context:
A global equipment manufacturer scaled AI across HR, operations, and customer service—but lacked centralized oversight.

Action Taken:

- Formed an AI Governance Board with stakeholders from Legal, Risk, IT, and Product

- Created a model inventory with usage, owner, risk level, and retraining cadence

- Required ethical impact assessments for all high-risk AI (e.g., hiring filters, safety alerts)

Outcomes:

- Improved regulatory readiness (e.g., GDPR AI disclosure compliance)

- Prevented deployment of biased hiring model with 14% gender skew

- Increased stakeholder confidence in AI from 54% to 89% in 12 months

Tools for AI Governance

1. Model Cards and Datasheets
Summarize purpose, training data, limitations, and known risks.

2. Explainability Frameworks
Use LIME, SHAP, or proprietary tools to visualize feature importance.

3. Bias Auditing Toolkits
Test models for disparate impact across gender, race, region, age, etc.

4. Model Registry Platforms
Track versions, owners, changes, and deployment status (e.g., MLflow, Azure ML, Seldon Core).

5. Decision Logs and Audit Trails
Ensure every AI-supported decision can be traced, questioned, and justified.

Compliance and Regulation

Emerging global regulations require stronger AI oversight:

- **EU AI Act**: Classifies and regulates high-risk AI with audit requirements

- **US SEC AI Disclosure Rules**: Demand transparency in AI-led financial decisions

- **GDPR Article 22**: Prohibits fully automated decisions that impact individuals without human recourse

- **CSRD (EU)**: Requires sustainability data, including AI-assisted reporting, to be verified

AI governance is essential not just for risk mitigation—but for **regulatory survival**.

Implementation Guidelines

1. **Create an AI Inventory**
   Document all current AI models, use cases, owners, and risk classifications.

2. **Establish Risk Tiers**
   Rank models by impact (e.g., safety, legal, customer, HR) and set review depth accordingly.

3. **Develop a Governance Policy**
   Define standards for fairness, transparency, and lifecycle management.

4. **Appoint Responsible Owners**
   Each model must have a business and technical steward.

5. **Involve Legal and Compliance Early**
   Design governance with regulation in mind—not as an afterthought.

6. **Educate All Stakeholders**
   Train employees on AI accountability, reporting protocols, and escalation channels.

Summary

Governance is the foundation for **scalable, sustainable AI**. It turns trust from a soft value into a hard requirement—ensuring every algorithm is accountable, fair, and aligned with both law and leadership.

In the next section, we'll explore how to build the **talent and culture** needed to drive AI success—not just through data scientists, but through a truly AI-fluent workforce.

8.2 Building AI Talent and Enterprise Fluency

Technology doesn't transform businesses—**people do**. While data, models, and platforms are critical, scaling AI across the enterprise ultimately depends on the **capabilities and mindset of the workforce**.

This means not only hiring data scientists, but also training operators, engineers, managers, and executives to work confidently with AI. It means creating **enterprise-wide AI fluency**, where everyone understands how AI works, where it adds value, and how to use it responsibly.

Without this foundation, even the best AI systems will underperform—or be ignored entirely.

The Talent Challenge in AI

As AI adoption grows, manufacturers face
several talent-related challenges:

- **Shortage of skilled data scientists and
  machine learning engineers**

- **Lack of AI understanding among
  business leaders and frontline
  workers**

- **Resistance to change from traditional
  departments**

- **Siloed teams with limited
  cross-functional collaboration**

- **Difficulty retaining AI talent in highly
  competitive markets**

To address these issues, organizations need a
dual approach: **build elite AI expertise** and
spread practical AI fluency across all roles.

Key Talent Roles in Scaled AI

Role	Description
Data Scientists	Design, train, and validate machine learning models
Machine Learning Engineers	Deploy models into production, manage APIs and infrastructure
Data Engineers	Build and maintain data pipelines and warehouses
AI Product Managers	Define AI use cases, align tech with business outcomes
Domain Experts	Provide context and validation for AI model outputs
AI Translators	Bridge the gap between technical teams and business units
Ethics & Risk Officers	Ensure compliance, fairness, and safety of AI applications

| AI Champions | Advocates within each function to promote adoption and innovation |

Enterprise AI Fluency: Beyond the Data Science Team

AI fluency means that non-technical professionals:

- Understand **what AI can and cannot do**

- Know how to **interpret AI outputs and recommendations**

- Are comfortable working with AI in daily tools (dashboards, decision assistants, etc.)

- Recognize and report **anomalies, bias, or unintended consequences**

- Contribute to the **continuous improvement** of AI systems

This fluency is essential across:

- **Operations and Maintenance**

- **Finance and Procurement**

- **Sales and Marketing**

- **R&D and Engineering**

- **HR and Talent Development**

- **Executive Leadership**

Case Study: Industrial AI Upskilling Program

Challenge:
A global machinery firm deployed AI models for scheduling, quality prediction, and procurement—but adoption lagged due to mistrust and misunderstanding.

Action Taken:

- Launched a 12-week AI fluency program for 1,500+ non-technical staff

- Offered role-specific modules (e.g., "AI for Maintenance," "AI in Sourcing")

- Created an internal AI Ambassador Network to answer questions and gather feedback

- Embedded AI literacy into onboarding and leadership training

Results:

- User adoption of AI tools rose from 38% to 84%

- 60+ new AI use cases proposed by non-technical teams

- Employee satisfaction with AI initiatives increased 2.4x

Talent Development Strategy

1. **Assess Current Capabilities**
   Use skills matrices and AI maturity models to identify gaps.

2. **Build Tiered Learning Paths**
   Design programs for basic fluency, applied skills, and advanced technical mastery.

3. **Partner with Academia and EdTech**
   Leverage MOOCs, bootcamps, and certificates from top AI providers.

4. **Create Internal AI Communities**
   Encourage knowledge-sharing through Slack channels, workshops, and hackathons.

5. **Reward Innovation and Adoption**
   Recognize employees who propose, improve, or scale AI solutions.

6. **Enable Career Growth in AI**
   Define internal AI career paths that allow mobility from operations, IT, or business roles.

AI Cultural Shifts

Scaling AI means creating a workplace culture that values:

- **Curiosity over control** – Encouraging experimentation with new tools

- **Collaboration over silos** – Building cross-functional teams

- **Transparency over black boxes** – Demystifying how AI makes decisions

- **Trust over fear** – Ensuring workers know AI is there to augment, not replace

- **Continuous learning** – Keeping up with evolving technology and best practices

Culture change starts from the top. Leaders must model openness to AI, encourage questions, and invest in capability building—not just technology budgets.

Strategic Partnerships for Talent Acceleration

- **Universities and technical schools**: Co-design programs aligned with enterprise needs

- **Industry associations**: Participate in sector-wide upskilling initiatives

- **Vendors and platform providers**: Train users on real-world AI tools

- **Startups and innovation hubs**: Gain exposure to emerging talent and fresh ideas

Summary

People are the multiplier—or the bottleneck—for AI success. By investing in both **deep expertise and broad literacy**, manufacturers can create a workforce that understands, improves, and embraces AI at every level.

In the next section, we'll focus on the **enterprise architecture** needed to support AI at scale—including cloud platforms, data lakes, model deployment tools, and system integration strategies.

8.3 Scalable AI Architecture and Model Operations (ModelOps)

No matter how advanced your AI models are, they're only as effective as the infrastructure supporting them. To scale artificial intelligence from pilot to enterprise, you need a **robust architecture**—one that enables model development, deployment, and monitoring across multiple functions, users, and environments.

This is the domain of **Model Operations (ModelOps)**—the set of tools and practices that turn isolated experiments into production-grade systems. ModelOps ensures AI systems are **repeatable, maintainable, observable, and reliable**, not just accurate in the lab.

Without it, even the most promising models risk collapse under the weight of technical debt.

The Complexity of Scaling AI Systems

Unlike traditional software, AI systems:

- Learn and evolve from data

- Depend on constantly changing external conditions

- Are probabilistic, not deterministic

- Require ongoing retraining and validation

- Introduce unique risks (bias, drift, explainability gaps)

As you scale from 3 to 30 to 300 models across an enterprise, complexity explodes. ModelOps is the discipline that keeps it all under control.

Key Components of Scalable AI Architecture

Layer	Core Functions
Data Layer	Ingest, clean, store, and access structured and unstructured data
Feature Store	Reusable library of model-ready variables for consistency and speed
Model Training	Frameworks for experimentation, hyperparameter tuning, and versioning
Model Registry	Central catalog of trained models, metadata, and approval status
Deployment Layer	CI/CD pipelines for deploying models to production (cloud, edge, apps)
Inference Layer	Real-time or batch prediction services integrated with business apps

Monitoring Layer	Track model performance, drift, accuracy, latency, and fairness
Governance Layer	Audit trails, access control, and compliance integration

All of these must be modular, interoperable, and scalable across teams and business units.

What Is ModelOps?

ModelOps focuses on the **full lifecycle of AI models**, from training to retirement. Key goals:

- Reduce time from model creation to deployment

- Ensure repeatability across environments

- Enable version control, rollback, and auditability

- Automate testing, approval, and rollout

- Monitor live models for drift, errors, or degradation

- Manage retraining, decommissioning, and incident response

ModelOps is to AI what DevOps is to software: a culture and toolset for **fast, safe, and sustainable delivery**.

Tools and Platforms for ModelOps

1. Data Platforms:
Databricks, Snowflake, Google BigQuery, Azure Synapse

2. Model Training Frameworks:
TensorFlow, PyTorch, Scikit-learn, Hugging Face, XGBoost

3. MLOps Platforms:
MLflow, Kubeflow, SageMaker, Azure ML, Vertex AI

4. Model Registry and Deployment:
Seldon, Tecton, BentoML, Fiddler

5. Observability Tools:
Arize AI, WhyLabs, Prometheus + Grafana (with custom metrics)

6. Orchestration:
Airflow, Prefect, Dagster for managing pipelines and retraining schedules

Case Study: AI Platform at Scale

Challenge:
A multinational manufacturer had 60+ models in production, each managed by different teams—creating duplication, inconsistency, and operational risk.

Solution:

- Centralized all models into a shared registry with metadata, owner, and status

- Implemented CI/CD for model deployment with test automation

- Set up model drift detection and auto-retraining triggers

- Created a single dashboard to monitor all model KPIs

Results:

- Model deployment cycle time dropped by 70%

- Incident response time for model failures improved by 85%

- $24M saved annually by reusing features and pipelines across teams

Best Practices for Scalable AI Infrastructure

1. **Design for Reusability**
   Build modular pipelines, reusable features, and standardized APIs.

2. **Treat Models as Products**
   Assign owners, SLAs, release notes, and feedback mechanisms.

3. **Automate Everything**
   From data ingestion to deployment to monitoring—minimize manual steps.

4. **Use Cloud-Native Tools**
   For scalability, elasticity, and multi-region redundancy.

5. **Create a Model Lifecycle Policy**
   Define triggers for retraining, archiving, rollback, or retrial.

6. **Secure Your AI Stack**
   Implement identity access management, encryption, and vulnerability scanning.

Key Metrics for ModelOps Maturity

Metric	What It Shows
Time to Deployment	Speed from dev to prod
Model Reuse Rate	Efficiency and standardization across teams
Retraining Frequency	Responsiveness to drift and market change
Incident Resolution Time	Operational resilience
Accuracy Degradation Rate	Model health over time
Fairness and Bias Score	Trustworthiness and ethical compliance

Tracking these KPIs helps demonstrate value, improve performance, and scale responsibly.

Summary

ModelOps is not a luxury—it's a necessity for industrial-scale AI. Without strong infrastructure, the risk of model failure, drift, and misuse rises with every deployment.

With it, AI becomes a **stable, scalable, and self-improving asset**—ready to power decision-making, automation, and innovation across the entire enterprise.

In the next and final section of this chapter, we'll bring it all together with a blueprint for scaling AI successfully—tying governance, talent, and architecture into one transformation roadmap.

8.4 Enterprise AI Scaling Blueprint and Maturity Model

Scaling AI isn't just about adding more models or tools—it's about evolving the entire organization. To do this, enterprises need a **structured roadmap** and a clear sense of where they are on the journey.

This section introduces a comprehensive **AI scaling blueprint** supported by a **maturity model** to benchmark progress. Together, they help leaders build alignment across governance, talent, and architecture—and drive sustained, measurable impact.

The 5 Stages of AI Maturity

Stage	Description
1. Experimentation	Isolated pilots, small teams, proof-of-concepts
2. Adoption	First use cases in production, early business value recognized
3. Integration	AI integrated into core systems and processes
4. Expansion	Multiple functions use AI, supported by central governance and infrastructure
5. Intelligence at Scale	AI embedded in culture, strategy, decision-making, and innovation

Each stage builds on the last—moving from technical curiosity to organizational transformation.

AI Scaling Blueprint: 6 Building Blocks

1. Leadership and Strategy

- Define a clear AI vision aligned to business goals

- Appoint executive sponsors and cross-functional champions

- Link AI metrics to strategic KPIs (e.g., revenue growth, margin improvement, ESG impact)

Checkpoint: Does every business unit understand how AI supports their success?

2. Governance and Ethics

- Create an AI governance framework (policy, standards, approvals)

- Conduct risk classification and model audits

- Ensure regulatory compliance (GDPR, CSRD, AI Act, etc.)

Checkpoint: Are all critical models documented, explainable, and accountable?

---

3. Talent and Skills

- Hire and retain specialized AI roles

- Upskill non-technical teams with AI literacy programs

- Create internal career pathways in AI and automation

Checkpoint: Are people at every level comfortable working with AI?

---

4. Enterprise Architecture

- Deploy cloud-native, scalable infrastructure

- Standardize data platforms, model registries, and pipelines

- Implement MLOps and model monitoring tools

Checkpoint: Can models be built, deployed, and maintained across functions with consistency?

---

5. Use Case Prioritization

- Identify high-ROI, low-risk starting points

- Build cross-functional squads for delivery

- Measure and publish outcomes to gain momentum

Checkpoint: Are use cases aligned to strategic goals and value tracked post-deployment?

---

6. Cultural Adoption

- Communicate successes through storytelling

- Celebrate teams driving AI progress

- Encourage ethical feedback and iteration from end users

Checkpoint: Is AI seen as a co-pilot—not a black box or threat?

Case Example: AI Scaling Across a Global Manufacturer

Year 1: Experimentation

- Launched 5 AI pilots in operations and maintenance

- Centralized data into a cloud lakehouse

- Defined AI governance policy with Legal and Compliance

Year 2: Integration

- Created a ModelOps platform and feature store

- Embedded AI KPIs into quarterly business reviews

- Trained 3,000+ staff in AI fluency via internal academy

Year 3: Intelligence at Scale

- 120+ models in production across 10 departments

- AI-assisted decisions drove $87M in net savings

- C-level dashboard integrated live AI recommendations

Measuring AI Maturity

Use a maturity scoring framework to assess where you are and where to go next:

Dimension	Score 1 (Low)	Score 5 (High)
Strategy	No AI strategy	AI embedded in corporate strategy
Governance	Ad hoc oversight	Formal model lifecycle controls in place
Talent	Skills gaps widespread	AI fluency across roles and levels
Architecture	Siloed or local infra	Scalable, enterprise-grade platforms
Use Case Value	Pilots with unclear ROI	Tracked value across deployed models
Culture	Fear or resistance	AI viewed as trusted, everyday tool

This diagnostic tool can guide quarterly or annual reviews of your AI transformation journey.

AI Scaling Pitfalls to Avoid

- **Scaling without standards**: Leads to chaos and inconsistent model performance

- **Focusing only on tools**: Neglects governance, skills, and business alignment

- **Lack of change management**: Causes resistance and poor adoption

- **No success measurement**: Undermines credibility and future investment

- **Ignoring bias and risk**: Erodes trust and creates compliance liabilities

AI Scaling Success Factors

- Strong **executive sponsorship** and budget commitment

- A central AI or **Innovation Office** to guide standards

- Empowered **domain teams** with data and tools

- Transparent measurement and **value communication**

- A clear **roadmap for AI literacy and talent development**

- Continuous improvement cycles with user feedback loops

Summary

Scaling AI is not just about technology—it's a coordinated effort across leadership, people, infrastructure, and culture. With a structured roadmap and maturity model in place, manufacturers can move confidently from pilots to platform—and from early wins to lasting transformation.

With Chapter 8 complete, we're now ready to enter the final chapter—bringing together all the learnings of this book into a practical, future-ready guide for the intelligent enterprise.

9.0 Introduction: Manufacturing in the Age of Intelligence

The industrial age was powered by steam. The digital age by silicon. Today, we stand at the dawn of a new era—one defined not by machines or microchips alone, but by **intelligence itself**.

Manufacturing is no longer just about producing things—it's about **learning systems that produce, improve, and adapt in real time**. Artificial intelligence is not simply a tool in this transformation—it is the foundation. It enables manufacturers to sense more, decide faster, and act smarter across every dimension of the enterprise.

This final chapter looks ahead—to the **opportunities, challenges, and responsibilities** that come with intelligent manufacturing. It asks not just what AI can do, but what we must do to lead with wisdom, courage, and clarity.

The Current Inflection Point

Over the past decade, manufacturers have invested in automation, digitization, and Industry 4.0 technologies. But AI takes this further—bringing **cognition to automation**, **prediction to planning**, and **adaptability to action**.

What once required intuition and decades of experience can now be modeled, simulated, and optimized in milliseconds. What once demanded rigid systems now favors flexible, autonomous networks. We are no longer just building factories—we are building **factories that think**.

And yet, this transformation is still young. Most organizations are still in the early stages of AI maturity. The pioneers are few. The possibilities, still largely untapped.

What the Future Holds

The next decade of intelligent manufacturing will likely include:

- **Fully autonomous factories** that operate with minimal human intervention

- **Hyper-personalized production** driven by real-time demand signals and predictive models

- **AI-designed products** tailored to usage patterns, environmental conditions, and individual preferences

- **Sustainable manufacturing systems** that optimize for carbon, waste, and circularity—not just cost

- **Synthetic workforces** combining human judgment, AI co-pilots, and robotic agents

- **Global supply networks** that self-reconfigure in response to disruptions or new opportunities

Manufacturers who embrace this evolution will thrive. Those who cling to legacy structures may struggle to survive.

Strategic Questions for the Road Ahead

1. **What will be our human advantage in an AI-first industry?**
   How do we empower workers to lead, interpret, and innovate with AI—not be replaced by it?

2. **How do we design for resilience, not just efficiency?**
   Can our AI systems anticipate and adapt to climate change, geopolitical shocks, and social shifts?

3. **How do we govern intelligence responsibly?**
   As decisions are delegated to machines, how do we ensure accountability, fairness, and trust?

4. **How do we scale equitably?**
   Can AI narrow the gap between large and small manufacturers, or will it widen the divide?

5. **What legacy will we leave?**
   Will intelligent manufacturing become a force for inclusion, sustainability, and prosperity—or another frontier for

exploitation?

These are not just operational questions. They are **moral and strategic imperatives**—requiring foresight, courage, and shared vision.

Summary

We began this journey exploring how AI reshapes the factory floor, the supply chain, the product, and the enterprise. As we conclude, we shift from implementation to imagination.

Because the future of manufacturing is not written yet.

It will be shaped by the leaders who rise today—with the tools of intelligence, the heart of industry, and the wisdom to build something truly transformative.

9.1 Emerging Trends That Will Shape the Next Decade

As artificial intelligence becomes the central nervous system of manufacturing, it's not operating in isolation. It's accelerating—and being accelerated by—a constellation of global trends, technologies, and market shifts. Together, they're reshaping how we design, build, distribute, and sustain everything from microchips to megastructures.

To lead in the age of intelligent industry, manufacturers must understand the forces driving the future.

1. From Mass Production to Mass Personalization

Customers today expect customized products, instant delivery, and eco-conscious manufacturing. AI enables this through:

- Real-time demand sensing

- Agile design platforms that adjust SKUs dynamically

- Predictive configuration based on user profiles or IoT feedback

- Autonomous production cells that switch between variants instantly

Example: A single apparel line could produce 10,000 unique combinations per week, guided by AI-driven fashion sentiment analysis and smart fabric printers.

2. AI + Robotics = Autonomous Manufacturing

While robotics have long handled repetitive tasks, AI is now unlocking true autonomy:

- Vision-guided robotics for complex object manipulation

- Multi-agent coordination in production cells and warehouses

- Cobots that adapt to human behavior and contextual cues

- Robotic process optimization driven by reinforcement learning

In the next decade, many factories will run 24/7 with **minimal human oversight**—monitored and optimized by centralized AI platforms.

3. Cyber-Physical Fusion and Digital Twins Everywhere

Digital twins—virtual replicas of machines, lines, or entire facilities—will become standard:

- AI-driven twins simulate outcomes in milliseconds

- Predict equipment failure, production bottlenecks, or environmental compliance risks

- Guide autonomous systems via constant feedback loops

As sensors become cheaper and more ubiquitous, the physical world will be mirrored—and governed—by real-time digital systems.

4. Edge AI and Smart Devices at Scale

As latency, bandwidth, and data privacy become limiting factors, intelligence will move closer to the machines:

- Edge AI will run quality checks, anomaly detection, and control loops locally

- Devices will make decisions without relying on cloud-based models

- Factory floors, shipping yards, and even field equipment will become **smart environments**

This decentralization enables **real-time reaction** and greater resilience—especially in remote or high-stakes applications.

5. Resilient, Adaptive Supply Chains

Global disruptions have exposed the fragility of traditional supply models. AI is ushering in:

- Multi-tier visibility across suppliers and logistics

- Predictive risk analysis (climate, conflict, cyber threats)

- Autonomous re-routing and fulfillment optimization

- Carbon-aware procurement to support ESG targets

The future supply chain will be **proactive, self-healing, and carbon-optimized**—not just cost-optimized.

6. Generative Design and Co-Creation with AI

AI is no longer just analyzing data—it's creating:

- Generative design platforms that evolve product geometry based on strength, weight, and material constraints

- AI-assisted CAD tools for engineers and non-experts alike

- Co-design interfaces where customers influence form and function via natural language or AR tools

Design becomes not a department—but a **collaboration between human insight and machine creativity**.

7. Green Manufacturing and Circular Economies

Sustainability will move from compliance to core strategy. AI will help:

- Monitor real-time emissions and energy use

- Optimize resource usage, water cycles, and waste flows

- Predict recyclability and end-of-life value

- Enable closed-loop product tracking and disassembly

Smart factories of the future will be **carbon-aware ecosystems**—capable of net-positive environmental contributions.

8. Workforce Evolution and Digital Human Twins

As automation expands, so will the role of humans:

- AI copilots will augment technicians, planners, and plant managers

- Digital human models will simulate ergonomic safety, training, and staffing needs

- Augmented reality and voice AI will support complex repair, onboarding, and auditing tasks

- Emotional and cognitive AI tools may one day support mental wellness and morale on the shop floor

This isn't the end of work—it's the **evolution of work with intelligent augmentation**.

9. AI Regulation and Ethics by Design

Governments and institutions are advancing regulatory frameworks to govern:

- Algorithmic accountability and transparency

- Worker surveillance and AI bias

- Digital sovereignty and cross-border data flows

- Mandatory sustainability and impact disclosures

Forward-looking manufacturers will integrate **compliance by design** and adopt open AI ethics policies before regulation catches up.

10. Platformization of Manufacturing

Just as cloud platforms transformed software, manufacturing will see:

- AI-powered operating systems for entire plants

- Digital marketplaces for parts, services, and capacity

- Integration of ERP, MES, and IIoT under unified intelligence layers

- Plug-and-play AI modules for scheduling, planning, and quality control

Manufacturers will increasingly buy **capability as a service**—not just software or hardware.

Summary

The next decade won't be shaped by a single technology—but by the **convergence of intelligent systems, sustainable strategies, and human-machine collaboration**.

Leaders who anticipate and act on these trends now will define the industrial frontier—not follow it.

In the next section, we'll examine the **risks and responsibilities** that come with this transformation—so that progress remains ethical, inclusive, and aligned with the values of humanity.

9.2 Risks, Ethics, and the Responsibility of Intelligence

As artificial intelligence reshapes manufacturing, it brings with it enormous power—but also profound responsibility. The same technologies that boost productivity and precision can also deepen inequality, displace workers, obscure accountability, and compromise human rights if misused or unchecked.

This section examines the **ethical dimensions and systemic risks** of intelligent manufacturing, and how leaders can shape a future where AI serves people—not the other way around.

1. Algorithmic Bias and Discrimination

AI systems trained on historical data can learn and amplify existing inequalities. In manufacturing, this can manifest as:

- **Biased hiring algorithms** that disadvantage underrepresented groups

- **Unequal safety recommendations** based on job roles or demographics

- **Supplier scoring models** that penalize smaller or minority-owned firms

Solution:
Use diverse, representative datasets. Conduct bias audits. Involve cross-functional and external reviewers. Make fairness a core model KPI.

2. Workforce Displacement and Dehumanization

AI-driven automation can lead to:

- **Job displacement**, especially among low-skill or repetitive roles

- **Erosion of human agency**, where workers become button-pushers for machine outputs

- **Morale decline**, as people feel replaced or surveilled

Solution:
Frame AI as augmentation, not replacement. Invest in reskilling. Redesign work to emphasize human strengths—judgment, creativity, empathy, adaptability.

3. Surveillance and Loss of Privacy

Smart cameras, wearables, and AI monitoring tools can cross into surveillance:

- Tracking workers' keystrokes, eye movements, and facial expressions

- Punishing minor "inefficiencies" without context

- Undermining trust and psychological safety

Solution:
 Set clear boundaries and policies. Prioritize privacy by design. Empower workers to understand, challenge, and opt out of surveillance tools where appropriate.

4. Loss of Explainability and Accountability

Black-box models in critical functions—like safety, quality control, or hiring—can create:

- Decisions no one can explain or contest

- Blame-shifting when things go wrong

- Regulatory breaches (e.g., GDPR, EU AI Act)

Solution:
Use interpretable models when stakes are high. Implement explainable AI (XAI) techniques. Require human oversight for sensitive decisions. Keep audit trails.

5. Deepening Global and Industrial Inequality

AI may benefit large enterprises disproportionately, as they:

- Have access to more data, compute, and talent

- Can afford full-scale platforms, retraining, and regulatory defense

- Set industry norms that smaller players struggle to meet

Solution:
Promote AI standardization, open tools, and public-private partnerships. Offer incentives and training for SMEs. Share successful templates.

6. Environmental Costs of Intelligence

Though AI can support sustainability, it also consumes:

- **Massive compute resources**, especially for training deep models

- **Energy-intensive hardware** in data centers and edge devices

- **Electronic waste** from rapidly obsolete smart equipment

Solution:
Adopt carbon-aware AI development. Use model pruning, low-power chips, and efficient architectures. Extend equipment life cycles through modularity.

7. Overreliance and Automation Bias

Humans may defer too readily to AI, leading to:

- Blind trust in flawed predictions

- Loss of critical thinking and challenge

- Dangerous failure modes when AI goes wrong

Solution:
Foster human-AI collaboration. Require regular model validation. Train users to ask, not just accept. Build interfaces that surface uncertainty, not just answers.

8. Intellectual Property and Data Ethics

AI models may:

- Inadvertently leak sensitive information

- Be trained on unauthorized or unlicensed data

- Replicate proprietary or personal content

Solution:
Enforce strict data lineage tracking. Use licensed, anonymized, or synthetic data. Monitor models for content misuse or leakage.

9. Societal Misinformation and Manipulation

AI in manufacturing can impact:

- **Public perceptions of safety and quality**

- **Regulatory narratives and lobbying**

- **Consumer trust in automation and AI-made goods**

Solution:
Lead with radical transparency. Publish ethics reports. Open models to third-party audits. Align with public interest and truth.

Principles of Responsible AI in Manufacturing

To build trust, protect stakeholders, and sustain innovation, responsible manufacturers should adopt:

- **Fairness:** No discrimination in access, outcomes, or opportunity

- **Accountability:** Clear human ownership of AI decisions

- **Transparency:** Explain how models work and are used

- **Security:** Protect systems, data, and outcomes from misuse

- **Privacy:** Minimize intrusive monitoring and inform users

- **Inclusivity:** Design with all users, geographies, and scales in mind

- **Sustainability:** Weigh environmental impact of AI choices

These principles are not just ethical—they are strategic. They future-proof your enterprise and differentiate your brand.

Summary

AI will reshape manufacturing—but how it reshapes society depends on the values we encode, the systems we build, and the culture we nurture.

Leaders must move beyond compliance to conscience—treating intelligence not only as a capability, but as a responsibility.

In the final section of this book, we'll present a call to action: how to lead intelligently, humanely, and boldly into the next industrial age.

9.3 Leading the Intelligent Enterprise: Final Reflections and Call to Action

Artificial intelligence is more than just another technological shift. It's a fundamental change in how decisions are made, how value is created, and how work is done. It challenges every assumption—about productivity, power, even purpose.

In this book, we've explored how AI is transforming the factory floor, the supply chain, the product, the workforce, and the entire enterprise. Now, we end not with a conclusion, but a **call to leadership**.

Because in this age of intelligence, success belongs not to the fastest adopters or the most advanced technologists—but to those with the **clearest vision, strongest values, and deepest understanding of people**.

The New Role of Leadership

In the intelligent enterprise, the leader is no longer the commander of resources—they are the **architect of learning systems**, the **custodian of ethics**, and the **translator of intelligence into impact**.

This new leadership role demands:

- **Curiosity** to ask better questions of AI

- **Humility** to listen to the data—and the people

- **Courage** to challenge biases and reject convenience

- **Conviction** to use AI for more than just profit

- **Clarity** to steer transformation amid complexity

Leadership is now about guiding machines and humans—together—toward a better way of working, living, and growing.

From Initiative to Identity

Too often, AI is treated as a project, an initiative, or a center of excellence. But intelligent manufacturing is not something you deploy—it's something you **become**.

It must be embedded in:

- **How you make decisions**

- **How you design your processes**

- **How you measure success**

- **How you treat people**

- **How you engage with the world**

The intelligent enterprise isn't a department or a platform—it's an identity. A way of thinking, acting, and leading.

Five Imperatives for the AI-Powered Manufacturer

1. Make Intelligence Everyone's Business
Democratize AI tools, skills, and decisions across every layer of the workforce. Turn curiosity into capability.

2. Move from Proof to Platform
Don't chase isolated pilots. Build reusable infrastructure and scalable governance that supports continuous innovation.

3. Lead with Transparency and Trust
Explain your AI systems. Audit their behavior. Be accountable to your workers, customers, and society.

4. Design for Resilience, Not Just Efficiency
Use AI to adapt, recover, and evolve—not just to optimize for today's conditions. Build for volatility.

5. Align with Human and Planetary Values
Let your AI strategies reflect your highest commitments—to equity, dignity, sustainability, and shared prosperity.

What the Future Demands

The factories of the future will be intelligent—but what will make them extraordinary is **the intelligence behind the intelligence**: the leaders who choose to put purpose before automation, people before platforms, and responsibility before convenience.

Manufacturers are uniquely positioned to shape this new world—not just with what they build, but with how they build it.

They can redefine the meaning of efficiency.
 They can model what ethical innovation looks like.
 They can make intelligence a public good—not just a competitive edge.

And in doing so, they can become more than successful.
 They can become **significant**.

Final Words

We have the tools.
We have the data.
We have the power.

Now, we must lead.

With intelligence.
With integrity.
And with imagination.

The future of manufacturing is not only smart—it
is ours to shape.

Glossary

AI (Artificial Intelligence)
The simulation of human intelligence in machines that are programmed to think, learn, and solve problems.

AI Co-Pilot
An AI tool that assists human workers by providing recommendations, insights, or automation in real time.

Algorithmic Bias
Unfair or prejudicial outcomes caused by flawed or unrepresentative training data in AI models.

AMR (Autonomous Mobile Robot)
A type of robot that can navigate and transport materials within a factory without fixed paths or human control.

Big Data
Large volumes of structured and unstructured data that require advanced methods to store, process, and analyze.

Cloud Computing
Internet-based computing where scalable resources such as storage, processing, and services are accessed remotely.

Computer Vision
AI techniques that enable machines to interpret and process visual data like images or video.

Digital Twin
A real-time digital replica of a physical asset, process, or system used for simulation and monitoring.

Edge AI
AI computing performed locally on hardware devices near the data source instead of in the cloud.

ESG (Environmental, Social, and Governance)
A set of sustainability and ethical standards used to evaluate corporate behavior and performance.

Feature Store
A centralized repository that stores, manages, and shares machine learning features for model training and inference.

Generative Design
A design method that uses AI algorithms to create optimal product models based on input constraints and goals.

Human-in-the-Loop (HITL)
A design approach where human judgment is

integrated into the AI decision-making loop for oversight or correction.

IIoT (Industrial Internet of Things)
 A network of interconnected sensors and devices used in industrial environments for real-time monitoring and control.

Inference
 The process by which an AI model makes predictions or decisions based on new input data.

Machine Learning (ML)
 A subset of AI that enables machines to learn from data and improve performance without explicit programming.

MES (Manufacturing Execution System)
 Software systems that manage and monitor production processes in real time on the factory floor.

Model Drift
 The degradation of an AI model's performance over time due to changing data patterns or external conditions.

ModelOps
 Practices and tools for managing the lifecycle of AI models, including deployment, monitoring, and retraining.

MLOps
 A broader operational framework that combines machine learning with DevOps for streamlined AI deployment and maintenance.

Predictive Maintenance
 AI-enabled forecasting of equipment failures before they occur to minimize downtime and reduce costs.

Reskilling
 Training employees with new skills to adapt to changing roles or technologies in the workplace.

Smart Factory
 A highly digitized and connected production facility that uses AI, IoT, and automation to self-optimize.

Supply Chain Resilience
 The ability of a supply chain to anticipate, prepare for, respond to, and recover from disruptions.

XAI (Explainable AI)
 A branch of AI that focuses on making model decisions transparent, understandable, and justifiable to humans.

Index

A

Accountability in AI, 276, 317
Additive manufacturing, 165
Agile production, 69, 171, 254
AI governance frameworks, 270–273
AI in finance, 206–210
AI in HR and workforce strategy, 212, 278
AI maturity model, 302–305
AI-powered supply chain, 128–135
Anomaly detection, 76, 133, 210, 248
Automation bias, 320
Autonomous material handling, 114–118
Autonomous mobile robots (AMRs), 115–116

B

Bias in AI, 267, 314–315
Big data integration, 44–49
Business case for AI, 24–26, 32
Buy vs. build strategy, 264

C

Carbon tracking and emissions reduction, 224–227
Change management for AI, 281–282
Cloud infrastructure, 260–261
Cobots (collaborative robots), 110–113
Computer vision systems, 104–108
Cybersecurity and AI, 262, 317

D

Data lakes, 46–47
Data pipelines, 250–252
Data privacy, 272, 318
Decision intelligence, 197, 203
Digital transformation roadmap, 298–301
Digital twins, 119–123
Displacement of workers, 313

E

Edge computing, 134, 174, 264
Energy optimization, 225–226
Enterprise architecture, 250–259
Ethical AI principles, 276, 314–319
Explainable AI (XAI), 272, 275, 315

F

Feature store, 252
Feedback loops in manufacturing, 47, 68
Forecasting with AI, 130–133, 207
Future of work, 176, 277, 319

G

Generative design, 172–173
Governance models (AI), 271–273

H

Human-AI collaboration, 110–113, 278–279
Human-in-the-loop, 272, 277

I

Indexing and traceability, 261, 268
Intelligent supply chain, 128–135

Intelligent factory, 124–127
IoT in manufacturing, 44–46
Infrastructure strategy, 250–259

L
Leadership in AI era, 324–327
Learning factories, 77, 127

M
Machine learning (ML), 26, 40–43
Manufacturing Execution Systems (MES), 44, 84
Model drift, 267
Model lifecycle, 252, 255, 258
ModelOps, 252–259

O
Operational optimization, 94–98
Organizational readiness, 278–281

P
Predictive analytics, 65–66, 133
Predictive maintenance, 61–66
Process automation, 94–100
Product design innovation, 170–174

Q
Quality assurance, 98–100
Quality prediction models, 97

R
Resilience in operations, 173, 221

Risk in AI scaling, 265–266, 314
Robotics, AI-enabled, 109–113

S
Scalability of AI systems, 250–259, 301–304
Smart logistics, 115–117
Smart sensors, 45
Strategic simulation with AI, 198–200
Supply chain visibility, 131

T
Talent development, 278–281
Training data, 41, 267
Transparency, 270, 274, 316

U
User adoption, 280, 284

V
Value tracking, 300, 303
Vision systems (AI), 104–108

W
Workforce transformation, 276–279

About the Author

Sayeed Siddiqui is a globally recognized authority on artificial intelligence and one of the most prolific authors of our time on the subject. With a body of work spanning dozens of acclaimed books, Sayeed has carved a unique path—bringing the power of AI to every major economic sector across the planet.

From healthcare to hospitality, finance to farming, law to logistics, energy to education—his writing fuses deep technical insight with real-world clarity. His mission is bold yet universal: to make advanced AI understandable, accessible, and transformational for industries, professionals, and policy makers alike.

Known for his elegant prose and comprehensive vision, Sayeed doesn't just document the AI revolution—he shapes it. His books serve as strategic roadmaps, used by executives, educators, engineers, and entrepreneurs around the globe. Whether it's decoding neural networks or reimagining entire supply chains, his work delivers clarity where others offer complexity.

When not writing, Sayeed mentors innovators, speaks at global forums, and guides enterprises through the age of intelligent transformation. His vision is unapologetically human: that technology, when wielded wisely, can elevate society, empower labor, and engineer a future that is fair, resilient, and free.

This book, *Manufacturing by AI*, is one more step in that journey—an offering to makers and thinkers everywhere, building a smarter world by design.

www.ingramcontent.com/pod-product-compliance
Lightning Source LLC
LaVergne TN
LVHW022331060326
832902LV00022B/3987